Social and Environmental Change

A Manual for Advocacy and Organizing

Bunyan Bryant

Social and Environmental Change:
A Manual for Advocacy and Organizing

by Bunyan Bryant

Published by:

Caddo Gap Press
1411 West Covell Boulevard
Suite 106-305
Davis, California 95616
(916) 753-1946

ISBN 0-9625945-3-9
LC# 90-085086

Table of Contents

-Continued on next page-

Table of Contents (continued)

Introduction

This manual is written for both students and community activists interested in changing social and environmental policies. It is organized into ten sections which cover various aspects of four key themes: 1) Ways of retrieving information to be used in organizing community groups; 2) understanding corporate and political power and the potential for working with it and using it; 3) the variety of ways action research information and the media can be used to facilitate change; and 4) procedures and prospects for community organizing in general.

Students interested in changing social and environmental policies from the grass-roots level on up have few opportunities to learn from an integrated body of knowledge assembled specifically to help them understand the use of power in social change. Thus, most learning about grass-roots organizing from a power orientation must come only from experience. The purpose of this manual is to help readers understand and combine theory and training activities with organizing experiences. It can be used by students or non-students to help community groups which seek policy changes through the use of power.

This manual is by no means designed to make students or community activists expert action researchers, community organizers, or change agents. Rather, it is designed to give an overview of some of the issues and skills involved in working for social and environmental change. To become expert at this kind of work necessitates considerable practice.

Why Is This Manual Important?

Present political, social, and economic cues appear to signal a dramatic shift in national environmental policies, thereby weakening public protection offered by the Environmental Protection Agency (EPA) as the federal government reduces the burden of regulation on industry. It is evident that we can't leave the protection of our environment to the government. We will have to take the initiative ourselves. There will always be a trade-off between environmental degradation and development -- but the more fundamental question is how much of one as opposed to the other? At present, it seems that the balance has drastically shifted toward development and the leasing of our most precious resources to the private sector.

To counteract such directions, we must prepare ourselves by developing a variety of skills to protect our communities, our ecosystems, and our environments. Relevant training in organizing skills must be brought to the classroom, and to community programs. With both commitment and a vision, we can do a lot to raise social and environmental issues and assure that they are dealt with in ways that impact our communities and surroundings positively.

Developing Understandings

This manual is designed to help people make corporations and governments more responsive to our environmental surroundings. Many corporations make efforts to influence the environment as minimally as possible; they should be commended and used as examples. In fact, several mutual funds, such as Working Assets and the Calvert Social Investment Funds, are concerned with both high profits and the social and economic impact of investment capital. Many brokers and investment professionals will identify such socially positive investment opportunities ; thus, investing according to one's conscience can be done. Conversely, those who consistently destroy our surroundings should be exposed, confronted, and organized against; our investments, both personal and governmental, should be withheld from such companies.

The 1990s will undoubtedly be tough, but exciting. Those of us who seek positive change must work with what we have -- and often that is not much. But if we are determined, we can make our world -- with all of its resources -- a better place in which to live.

Ten Two-Hour Sessions

It should take about ten two-hour sessions to effectively use this manual. Sessions can, if desired, be combined into a one-weekend seminar, or parts of sessions can be used independently.

In addition to this manual, one other resource is important for doing action research: *How to Read A Financial Report,* available from Merrill, Lynch, Pierce, Fenner, and Smith, Inc., One Liberty Plaza, 165 Broadway, New York. This publication is free. It is particularly useful for sessions four and five in this manual.

Another useful resource is *Looking at Sixty Minutes.* This is a 50-minute, 3/4-inch video tape, number 631V, that can be ordered from: Michigan Media, The University of Michigan, 400 Fourth Street, Ann Arbor, Michigan 48109-4816, (313) 764-5360.

Session Number One: Getting Started

Objectives of the Session

To explain seminar expectations, goals, and objectives.

To share background experiences, knowledge, opinions, and different beliefs and values.

To provide opportunities to get to know one another for subsequent team building.

To encourage listening to opinions, beliefs, and issues that may differ from your own.

To explain the training manual and design flow.

Design Flow in Minutes

5 minutes Agenda review.

20 minutes Introduction to manual, expectations, and requirements.

15 minutes Question and answer session.

10 minutes Break.

10 minutes Goals and getting to know one another.

10 minutes Activity: From the following pages pick one button you like and one you dislike. Now duplicate these buttons on a sheet of paper. Make them large and attractive. If you do not like any of the buttons, then make your own.

30 minutes Activity: Divide yourselves into groups of four and introduce yourselves. Each person is to take five minutes to speak, indicating why he or she chose a particular button. Others are to engage in active listening; they are to ask questions for clarification only.

20 minutes Total group discussion: What do we have in common with others in the group? What are some of the differences? How did we react to each other's ideas? Can we interact without stereotyping each other?

More About the Buttons

Buttons are often clear statements of peoples' preferences or political ideologies--part of one's identity. And people read them. It is an effective way of ascertaining what's on peoples' minds or what the major issues are at a given time in society. On the following two pages are dozens of buttons, some of which go back several years in history. Pick one button that you identify with and one that you do not identify with--or, if none of the ones below are appropriate, then make up your own. Duplicate the buttons on a large sheet of paper. You may want to decorate them. Take masking tape and attach them to your chest so they can be easily seen by others. Be prepared to get into groups of four and share reasons for your choice of buttons. Others

should listen, ask questions of clarification, and discuss issues without making value judgments. By doing so, participants may gain greater clarity of values and preferences. This exercise may be risky for some. If so, then don't do it. The exercise is designed to help you grow both personally and politically.

Homework

The questionnaire which follows the two pages of buttons is designed to help you obtain clarity on your own values by getting in touch with your background and how it influences your behavior and outlook on social and environmental change. Try to be honest and candid; the quality of the discussion will depend upon your honesty and willingness to share questionnaire results. Also read the first concept paper on *Action Research* and the *Ten Theses on Power Structure* which follow.

Figure 1	
Share of Wealth Held by the Richest 1 Percent	
Year	Share of Wealth Held by 1 Percent of U.S. Adults or Families
1810	21.0
1860	24.0
1870	27.0
1900	26.0--- 31.0
1922	31.6
1929	36.3
1933	28.3
1939	30.6
1945	23.3
1949	20.8
1953	27.5
1956	26.0
1958	26.9
1962	27.7
1963	31.6
1965	29.2
1969	24.9
1983	34.3

Source: Batra, R. *The Great Depression of 1990.* New York: A Dell Book, 1987, p. 133.

Sample Political Butttons

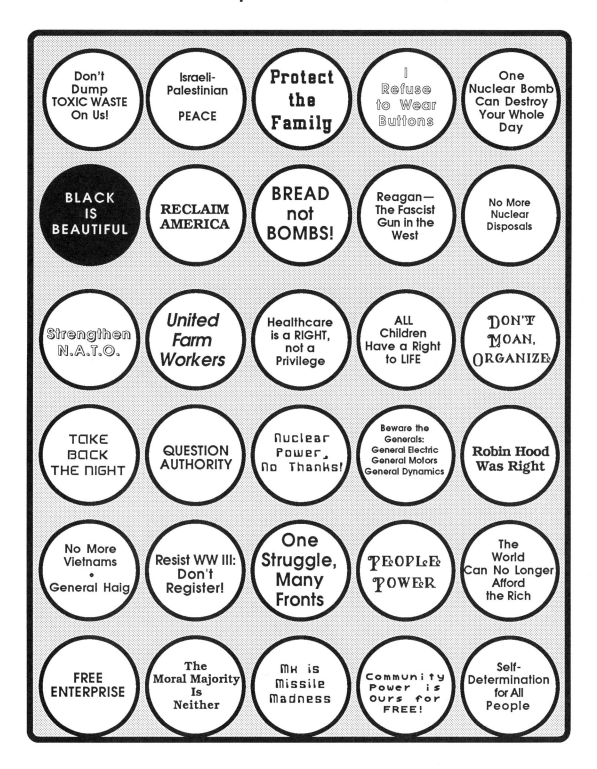

(Button design by Tania Hurie)

More Sample Political Buttons

Make Nestle's Stop Quick

NO NUKES!

Nuclear Power — Safe and Clean

How Dare You Presume I'd Like to be Young!

Wearing Buttons Is Not Enough

I Brake for Animals

Resist Racism

Bell is a Phony

Sexism is a Social Disease

Hiroshima — Never Again!

ERA: No Time Limit on Equality

The World We Build Will Be Our Own

RECALL REAGAN

Reagan in '84

This Is A UNION MADE Button

U.S. Out of El Salvador

SOLAR POWER

Sure I'm a Capitalist

Sure I'm a Marxist

We Were Here Long Before Columbus

HOMOPHOBIA Is a Social Disease

Security = Strong Armed Forces

MAKE LOVE NOT WAR

University of Michigan

A SMILE BUTTON

War Is Good Business — Invest Your Son!

A Woman's Place Is In the House

Let Them Eat Jelly Beans...

FREEZE NUCLEAR WEAPONS

CHOICE is the Issue • Abortion Rights

(Button design by Tania Hurie)

Questionnaire

This questionnaire was constructed by the Foundation for Student Communication, Inc., publishers of *Business Today Magazine*. It has been modified for purposes of this manual.

1)   Describe the geographical area in which you live (your permanent address) --you may choose more than one:

<table>
<tr><td colspan="2" align="center">*Section of United States*</td><td align="center">*Nature of Location*</td></tr>
<tr><td>___northeast</td><td>___northwest</td><td>___urban</td></tr>
<tr><td>___southeast</td><td>___west coast</td><td>___rural</td></tr>
<tr><td>___midwest</td><td>___southwest</td><td>___suburban</td></tr>
</table>

2)   Describe yourself politically--you may choose more than one:

<table>
<tr><td>___conservative</td><td>___strong republican</td><td>___very active politically</td></tr>
<tr><td>___somewhat conservative</td><td>___moderate republican</td><td>___moderately active politically</td></tr>
<tr><td>___moderate</td><td>___independent</td><td>___not very active politically</td></tr>
<tr><td>___somewhat liberal</td><td>___moderate democrat</td><td>___I vote, that's about it</td></tr>
<tr><td>___liberal</td><td>___strong democrat</td><td>___politically inactive</td></tr>
<tr><td>___don't know</td><td>___don't know</td><td>___don't know</td></tr>
<tr><td>___other (explain)</td><td>___other (explain)</td><td>___other (explain)</td></tr>
<tr><td>_____</td><td>_____</td><td>_____</td></tr>
<tr><td>_____</td><td>_____</td><td>_____</td></tr>
</table>

3)   Overall, how much trust and confidence do you have in the following industries?

	a great deal	some	very little	none	no opinion
a) auto manufacturing	___	___	___	___	___
b) aerospace companies	___	___	___	___	___
c) electric & gas utilities	___	___	___	___	___
d) oil companies	___	___	___	___	___
e) advertising agencies	___	___	___	___	___
f) drug companies	___	___	___	___	___
g) telephone companies	___	___	___	___	___
h) food companies	___	___	___	___	___
i) insurance companies	___	___	___	___	___
j) retail chain stores	___	___	___	___	___
k) chemical companies	___	___	___	___	___
l) banks	___	___	___	___	___
m) high tech companies	___	___	___	___	___
n) timber companies	___	___	___	___	___
o) coal companies	___	___	___	___	___

(Continued on next page)

Questionnaire (continued)

4) Overall, how do you rate the ethics of corporate executives?

___excellent ___good ___only fair ___poor ___no opinion

5) Do you feel that all, most, some, or no businesses overcharge for the products or services they provide?

___all ___most ___some ___none ___no opinion

6) Overall, how much trust and confidence do you have in:

	a great deal	some	very little	none	no opinion
a) large corporations	___	___	___	___	___
b) small businesses	___	___	___	___	___

7) How much power do corporations wield within our political system?

___a great deal ___some ___very little ___none ___no opinion

	agree strongly	agree somewhat	not sure	disagree somewhat	disagree strongly
8) The government should impose regulations governing wages and prices.	___	___	___	___	___
9) Large corporations are too powerful and have too much influence over both domestic and foreign policies.	___	___	___	___	___
10) Large corporations could do a better job in protecting our environment against pollution.	___	___	___	___	___
11) There is nothing wrong with large corporations if they would just act more responsively to people and to environmental conditions.	___	___	___	___	___
12) Large corporations have done more good for this country than harm, and they should be protected against policies that make life difficult for them.	___	___	___	___	___

(continued on next page)

Questionnaire (continued)

		agree strongly	agree somewhat	not sure	disagree somewhat	disagree strongly
13)	Business leaders do everything they can to make a profit, even if it means losing their ethical standards.	___	___	___	___	___
14)	The corporate sector has a moral conscience -- it is motivated by more than the goal of maximizing profits.	___	___	___	___	___
15)	A breakup of corporations would lower prices due to increased competition among smaller firms.	___	___	___	___	___
16)	Most corporations want to correct the pollution they cause.	___	___	___	___	___
17)	If meaningful changes are to occur in underdeveloped countries, it will result from the activities of multi-national corporations.	___	___	___	___	___
18)	For the good of the country, many of our largest corporations should be broken up into smaller companies.	___	___	___	___	___

19) How do you rate the performance of businesses in the following areas?

	good	fair	poor	no opinion
a) improving urban areas	___	___	___	___
b) supporting higher education	___	___	___	___
c) controlling pollution	___	___	___	___
d) raising living standards	___	___	___	___
e) creating jobs	___	___	___	___
f) hiring minorities	___	___	___	___
g) producing quality products	___	___	___	___
h) hiring women	___	___	___	___

20) In your opinion, does this country need more or less government regulation of business than we have now?

___more government regulation   ___less government regulation
___same as now   ___no opinion

(continued on next page)

Questionnaire (Continued)

21) Relatively speaking, how much is each of the following to blame for our country's current economic slump? (please rate 1 to 5, 1 being most blameworthy, 5 being least blameworthy)

	1	2	3	4	5
a) government regulation	___	___	___	___	___
b) government deficits	___	___	___	___	___
c) business/management	___	___	___	___	___
d) labor unions	___	___	___	___	___
e) excessive taxation	___	___	___	___	___
f) the fed's monetary policy	___	___	___	___	___

22) Do you feel that most corporations are very truthful, fairly truthful, or not truthful in the information they release to the media?

___very truthful   ___fairly truthful   ___not truthful   ___no opinion   ___don't know

23) In your opinion, does this country need more or less government regulation of business in the following areas?

	more regulation	less regulation	same as now	no opinion
a) pollution control	___	___	___	___
b) product safety	___	___	___	___
c) pricing of products	___	___	___	___
d) business profits	___	___	___	___
e) salaries and wages	___	___	___	___
f) corporate acquisitions and mergers	___	___	___	___
g) international trade	___	___	___	___

24) Corporations have been charged with making both illegal political campaign contributions and unethical or question able payments to officials of foreign countries. Do you feel that most businesses, some businesses, relatively few businesses, or no businesses make illegal and unethical contributions?

	illegal political contributions	unethical payments to foreign officials
most businesses	___	___
some businesses	___	___
few businesses	___	___
none	___	___
no opinion	___	___

(Continued on next page)

Questionnaire (Continued)

25) How can businesses accomplish the goal of ensuring equal employment opportunities for minorities and women?

___affirmative action plans   ___job training programs
___support government programs   ___other (please specify)

_____

_____

26) Overall, how do you rate businesses' efforts to hire and promote minorities and women?

___excellent   ___good   ___satisfactory   ___poor   ___no opinion

27) What should I do about large corporations that pollute, destroy natural resources, and exploit workers here and abroad?

Please place a check under the heading that best represents your point of view.

	Yes	Maybe	No
Work for them and change them from the inside.	___	___	___
Organize against them and fight to resist their industrial policies that destroy our natural resources and exploit people who work for them.	___	___	___
Join them and try to present their point of view.	___	___	___
Push for more legislation to protect the environment.	___	___	___

[End of Questionnaire]

Results of the questionnaire will be discussed during Session Number Two.

Learning from Differences

As mentioned before, you probably view society from your own history, background, and tradition. Parents and friends affect you in subtle and not so subtle ways. Values and attitudes picked up in early years often stay with you, helping to determine your world view. The button exercise and the questionnaire are designed to help you clarify your values about corporations and society in general. We can expect differences of opinion and beliefs, and we expect to learn from such differences.

As you go through this manual, keep in mind how your personal background influences both your attitude and behavior. Thousands of people every day are confronting old behavior patterns and making changes as reflected in voluntary simplicity, alternative lifestyles, and organizational forms of democratic management and worker-consumer co-ops. As you go through this manual, confront yourself and your friends.

Introducing Action Research

In preparation for Session Two we will now focus on action research as a means for retrieving data on corporations, thus enabling us to make a litmus test of fair play. Following are two items for you to read prior to Session Two: a concept paper on *Action Research* and a document entitled *Ten Theses on Power Structure Research*.

CONCEPT PAPER I: Action Research

We are the most powerful country in the world. Although the United States constitutes about 6 percent of the world's population, utilizing about 30 percent of the world's resources, it is responsible for about 30 to 40 percent of the world's pollution. Our history is characterized by growth and productivity and by science and technology for improving the health and living conditions of people throughout the world. Yet, in our quest for knowledge and productivity, we have also caused a great deal of suffering by destroying our land and polluting our air and water--the very life forces that are so important to us. We are not intentionally self-destructive, but the by-products of production in our pursuit of growth policies are mainly responsible.

Often we feel it is beyond us to influence the growth policies of this country. Even though institutions are large and complex, they seldom respond adequately to the needs of local communities. We feel alienated and disenfranchised by the concentration of power in the hands of a few corporate barons who, in turn, influence both our domestic and foreign policies.

How do we reassert ourselves? How do we influence certain growth policies? How do we get institutions to become more responsible for the condition of the environment? These questions bring us to the reasons for engaging in action research. But first, action research should be defined.

Action research is the intentional gathering of information to be used to organize individuals and groups in the community for collective action. Information is gathered on the strengths and weaknesses of antagonists, then such information is used in planning action strategies for social or policy changes. More importantly, action research helps to ensure success. This success is consciously used to build a strong organization. Community groups and individuals can take charge of their own lives by:

1) Identifying individuals and organizations responsible for environmental and social dehumanization--we must come to know and understand more adequately the forces that are causing intolerable conditions;

2) Locating vulnerable points within the institution under investigation, to give us leverage for challenging and making them more responsive to our needs--often we feel that corporations are so powerful that we can never influence them. We must remember, however, that corporate America spends billions of dollars every year painting a positive image of its activities. The public image of a corporation is important for sustaining profits and attracting competent employees.

3) Raising our consciousness about interrelations of corporate and governmental power--we should support those activities responsive to our needs and make known activities of government and corporate interactions that are detrimental. The more we can raise the consciousness of society at large, the more power we can exert upon corporations which are derelict in their responsibilities.

We should not be afraid to do action research. All too often research has been mystified; it was something that only highly trained academicians could do. But social and environmental groups all over the country are doing varying forms of research to help keep those at the center of decision-making power honest. Ralph Nader has called for the building of alternative institutions, with one function being to research corporations--so as not to be dependent upon the data they give us. Highlander, a school which trains community people, has engaged people in researching land ownership patterns of coal companies in Kentucky and Tennessee. The Corporation Information Center of the National Council of Churches has done corporate research for a number of years, confronting corporations on their investment portfolios and their policies on affirmative action. These are examples of only a few organizations involved in making institutions more accountable through action research.

In order to have an impact it's important that we do a most thorough job on our homework. To get angry about research findings and expressing that anger publicly can be more of a detriment. Having an impact in a given direction means having facts together in a well-organized manner, and being able to articulate them. It means probing and getting beneath surface flaws, to get at root causes of the problems under study. Inability to control one's anger before completing one's research could cause one to lose the necessary power that is important to influence desired outcomes.

Correct information applied to the correct situation is power. By itself, information is a neutral resource, but like most resources in our society, how it is used, and to what end, and who benefits, is political in character. At universities, research is funded primarily by the government and powerful interest groups, to further their own growth, efficiency, and goals. Research is supposed to be value-free and objective in university circles, but that is basically a myth. Academicians who refuse to recognize the value centralities of academic research or the social context within which they work are a part of the social and environmental problems we face today.

We assume that those involved in doing action research must ultimately answer the question, "Whose side am I on?" Federal and corporate budgetary cuts make Americans more class conscious; it is those at the lower reaches of society who undoubtedly suffer the most; it is women, minorities, the aged, and youth of our society who desperately need jobs and a chance for social dignity. Research is being done on people, rather than for them. Such information is used to make policy to maintain the status quo. Further, American social science has traditionally studied individuals, institutions, and society as it functions or as it is structured. Within this context, the study becomes one of examining flaws within the system, rather than the structural or functional context out of which these flaws originate.

Community organizations need to make priorities. Every issue is not important to research. There is neither the time nor the money. Priorities should be placed upon researching those issues to help build a power constituency or organization. This clearly separates this kind of research from the research done by investigative reporters, or by Ralph Nader, or by academicians. With respect to the first, investigative reporters have a vested interest in exploring anyone's closet for skeletons to make public. Ralph Nader is more discriminate, in that he is more interested in issue-oriented research that will have a significant impact upon society. In both instances investigative reporters and Nader feel that, given the information, people will respond to correct the situation. The kind of research done by universities is often too abstract and thus fails to be helpful to community organizations. Community organizations are seldom interested in exploring institutional or personal corruption for the sake of making that information known; they are more interested in those issues that make it easier for them to organize and build and develop an organization. Here are some of the advantages and uses of action research, as presented in a lecture in 1977 by Barry Greever at the Midwest Academy in Chicago:

A. It helps to evaluate possible strategies for change. The more information known about an organization under investigation, the easier it is to make effective decisions regarding strategies to use.

B. It helps to define intermediate victories. Often, people being organized are the disenfranchised and alienated, who have experienced little success in life. They will not be attracted to a losing organization, and therefore it is important that new achievements, even though small, be made explicit so they may experience feelings of success.

C. It helps to analyze strengths and weaknesses of the enemy to be used in developing strategy and tactics, in order to tell where to put the pressure. ("The enemy" is a term seldom used in social science literature, probably because it separates groups and makes them vulnerable to attack.) Action research helps define more specific step-by-step action plans. These more specific steps are usually embodied within the larger strategy for change.

D. It helps to neutralize the opposition. A judge or a political figure may have certain biases. How do you obtain a different judge, etc., and one who may be more sympathetic?

E. It helps to develop leadership. In some cases it is appropriate to involve community people so they may learn the skills of action research. Developing leadership is important so organizations will have a number of skilled leadership people to help carry on.

F. It keeps people involved and interested. Information retrieved from action research is used to bring about change and keeps people interested and involved.

An action researcher often spends considerable time uncovering concealed information. Finding deliberately concealed information is rather difficult, requiring hours to research files, which may or may not produce desired results. It takes extraordinary stick-to-itiveness, which often determines the difference between success and failure. Perseverance is anchored in the assumptions action researchers make about human nature: that in a highly affluent society, there is probably always someone working against the public good. Political payoffs, using privileged information to increase profits, and other illegal machinations, can frequently be found in the daily newspapers.

Another assumption that action researchers make is that illegal acts cannot be covered up indefinitely. People involved in questionable activities sometimes boast about their exploits to friends and acquaintances, or carelessly file incriminating information in the public domain. Cues to uncovering illegal exploits are always there. You have to be painstakingly thorough to make sure that the information is accurate.

Facts should be checked with a variety of sources several times to make sure they are correct. Charm is less important than a willingness to think carefully about the facts and to frame issues based upon the research. As researchers, we must assume that the information wanted exists and can be retrieved.

A considerable number of state and local governments adopt a substantial body of law and, in some cases, it is specifically designed to keep investigative reporters, action researchers, and others at arm's length. Policy decisions are made behind closed doors. Records of mismanagement or illegal activity, which could be used to make acts against the state or mismanagement known, are kept from reporters, researchers, and the public. Such laws do present an interesting dilemma: Should a researcher knowingly and willfully break a law to gain access to information that would expose corporate or governmental corruption? Should reporters or researchers be deceptive in retrieving information from their sources? Does breaking a minor law to expose those breaking a greater law justify the means? Many fundamental techniques of researchers involve actions that could be called dishonest, fraudulent, immoral, and even illegal. Yet, if the researcher is not dishonest, the story would never appear about the wrong-doings of public officials. Those officials would continue their crimes against the state. These are questions that action researchers have to answer for themselves, and they must be willing to suffer the consequences if their conscience requires them to be dishonest. These are questions which will be raised consistently as this manual is read and discussed by participants.

Although it is a personal decision, researchers themselves should be beyond reproach. To be in this line of work, researchers should be Mr. or Ms. "Good Citizen." A researcher who is vulnerable to past or present activities runs the risk of destroying his or her credibility. Researchers have to remember that it's a two-way street, that antagonists are often more powerful, with more resources at their disposal to discredit or defang the researcher.

As part of your homework, answer the following questions before moving on to read the ten theses on power structure research:

1) How does action research differ from traditional academic research and investigative reporting?

2) What are the functions of academic research? How does it relate to empowerment?

3) What are some of your feelings about doing action research? How would you explain this to your parents,

who may depend upon corporations for their existence and support for you?

Ten Theses on Power Structure Research

The following "Ten Theses on Power Structure Research" are helpful to the action researcher. Power structure research differs in its use of research information. Information is often used for dissemination purposes, but in action research, information is used to organize constituencies to build strong organizations. Information is only worthwhile if it can be used to enhance the strength of the organization for social change.

1. The very complex nature of modern technological society compels the U.S. power structure to produce a continuous flow of accurate data on every aspect of human endeavor. It is safe to assume, therefore, that the information needed for an investigation of any segment of U.S. society is available somewhere, in some form.

2. For every component of U.S. society, there exists an *Information Infrastructure* (I/I), designed to produce the data required for the successful performance of that component. This infrastructure will ordinarily consist of government agencies, university research centers, professional organizations, trade associations, special libraries, and companies which publish trade books and periodicals.

3. The first task of the researcher is to identify the I/I in his/her field. The quickest way to do this is to locate the trade journals and newspapers which service this field. These publications usually report on the activities of the other parts of the I/I (or carry their advertising). Several standard reference books can also be used to identify I/Is.

4. Having identified the I/I, the next task is to insert oneself into its regular operations. This ordinarily involves subscribing to trade publications, joining professional organizations, attending trade shows and conferences, etc. Successful penetration of the I/I in any field will normally provide the researcher with access to most of the information sources used by this component of society.

5. In all dealings with the I/I, it is necessary to protect oneself as a legitimate member of the corporate state -- always remember that as a citizen of the United States, you are *entitled* to have the information you request. Credibility of this sort is achieved through a variety of techniques, including: use of printed stationery, the pretense that a letter has been typed by a secretary, aggressive telephone calling, etc.

6. In every large organization, there is someone who has jurisdiction over each kind of activity and/or each area of knowledge. Before requesting specialized information from an organization, therefore, the researcher should identify the person responsible for that kind of data, and address her/him directly. Pinpointing the right person for a specific request is a good way to establish credibility in the field, and will usually speed up response time from the organization.

7. Every field of activity has its unique jargon--a knowledge of which is required for any extended conversation with people in this field. Examination of trade publications and contact with friends in the field will usually provide a working knowledge of this jargon. Mastery of professional jargon is also one sure way of establishing credibility in any field.

8. Every subgroup in the population recognizes certain stereotypes of "correct" dress and behavior for people within its sphere of operations. The more one conforms to these stereotypes, at least superficially, the easier it will be to overcome initial obstacles in obtaining information. While individualistic dress and hair styles may be an appropriate way to establish autonomy within an organization, they are not appropriate for a researcher who seeks to penetrate a group to which he does not belong. Oppressive or not, short hair and neat clothes will usually evoke a better response from "Establishment" organizations than long hair and informal dress. Similarly, when talking to workers and GI's, work clothes will be more appropriate than a jacket and tie.

9. After all published sources of information on a subject have been exhausted, it is essential to make direct contact with knowledgeable people inside the field you are investigating. Interviews, informal conversations, and even telephone conversations are important techniques for developing a "feel" for a subject, and for understanding the ideology of people in the field. Access to newspaper or magazine credentials will be particularly helpful in this regard. Most people, and most organizations, do not want the public to believe that they are secretive and remote; if you have trouble getting an interview, try to have someone with "Establishment" credentials make a fuss about secrecy, as this will sometimes succeed in softening up the resistance.

10. When engaging in power structure research, always seek to work "with the grain" instead of against it. If old friends or relatives have joined an "Establishment" organization, do not be embarrassed to seek their help (even if you disagree with their politics). If people you know own stock in the corporation under investigation, try to use their proxy to attend stockholder meetings and to obtain other benefits. If anyone on the research team has some claim (legitimate or otherwise) to "Establishment" credentials, these should be used to the fullest advantage; most Americans have inordinate respect for white collar professionals (especially lawyers, doctors, librarians, and college professors) and will be particularly cooperative in answering their requests for information. A friendly professor who will let you use his letterhead when writing for information is a particularly valuable ally, and should be enlisted on the project. Always take advantage of all opportunities to advance your knowledge of a subject.

The above 10 points were taken from: *NACLA Research Methodology Guide*. New York: Congress on Latin America, 1971.

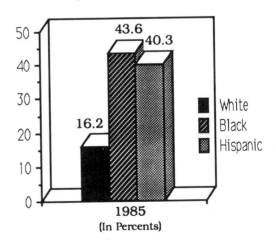

Figure 2

Families with Female Householder as a Percent of All Poor Families

48%

■ Women
▨ Other

1985

Poverty Status of Persons by Race

43.6 40.3

16.2

■ White
▨ Black
▨ Hispanic

1985
(In Percents)

Source: U. S Department of Commerce, Bureau of the Census. *Poverty in the United States 1985*. Washington, D.C.: U. S. Government Printing Office, 1987.

Session Number Two: Types of Research

Objectives of Session

To articulate the difference between traditional academic research, action research, and investigative reporting.

To provide opportunities to explore your own values and opinions about yourself and institutionally based power in America.

Design Flow in Minutes

5 minutes Agenda Review.

10 minutes Excitement Sharing: This activity is designed to enable group members to share positive and exciting events from their personal lives--the arrival of a new baby or the purchase of a new automobile are examples of such events. Positive statements about individuals in the group may be shared as well. This kind of sharing helps set a good, upbeat tone for the various sessions.

45 minutes Discussion of questionnaire answers in trios--discuss the first 12 questions.

10 minutes Break.

20 minutes Lecture/discussion on "Action Research."

15 minutes Discussion of questions on page 13.

10 minutes Evaluation.

Homework

At the same time that we explore ways of doing action research, you should become familiar with conflict theory. By understanding conflict, you may be able to obtain a greater insight into political and/or conflict messages inherent in the variety of buttons displayed earlier in this manual. In the next reading, Concept Paper II, two basic approaches to change are discussed.

Concept Paper II:
Social and Environmental Conflict -- Theory and Analysis.

Although conflict is defined as contending parties or interest groups competing over scarce resources, goals, values, traditions, culture, and power, it can also be defined as a struggle over class dominance, whereby the working class and the poor attempt to gain control over both economic and political institutions to put an end to class exploitation and alienation fostered by elite groups. It is clear that it is a part of the human experience; it is a part of our socialization process, and it will probably be with us forever. Although conflict can be observed at every level of society and although it may be controversial, it is responsible for many changes in society--both positive and negative. And in order for us to use conflict effectively, we will have to view it in positive terms; we will have to view it as an opportunity to make constructive social change.

In this paper, two basic theoretical approaches to social change are discussed--Conflict Theory I and Conflict Theory II. While the former represents reformist incremental change within the context of consensus agreement based upon the basic institutions and values of society, the latter is a theory of fundamental change that confronts and questions societal contradictions; it confronts and questions privileged positions and the basic values upon which our institutions are built. While the distinctions of these two theories as presented in this manual are by no means conclusive, they do help us to an extent to glean an understanding of our own actions and the actions of others; they do help us understand many of the societal forces at play.

Conflict Theory I

Growing out of the more liberal-conservative tradition, Conflict Theory I scholar-activists claim that class formations are not necessarily related to owners and nonowners of production. They feel that social class divisions are more complex. Money, lineage, status, kind of job, child-rearing patterns, places of vacation, kinds of food, schooling, social registers, places of residence, political attitudes, kinds of mental illnesses and where they are treated, and a whole host of other variables are used to determine social class. Social class cannot be simply relegated to the "haves" and "have-nots," or to owners and nonowners of production.

To transcend class boundaries within the context of the Conflict Theory I model, working class people and minorities have found collective expression in special interest groups and forums, such as labor and trade unions, school desegregation efforts, community control of schools, welfare, and the civil rights movements. The collective expressions mentioned above are attempts to improve the social class status of such groups through highly prescribed institutionalized means. Although there are social inequities, such inequalities can be overcome within a pluralist context by aggrieved groups organizing to champion their self-interests. Social class cannot be simply relegated to the "haves" and the "have-nots."

While such interest groups attempt to organize to obtain more of society's rewards and improve their status or social class position, a number of special interests, such as abortion and anti-abortion groups, environmental and pro-development groups, pro-nuclear and anti-nuclear groups, school prayer and separation of church and state groups, creation and evolution groups, fail to consider in any meaningful way social class differences, let alone challenge the assumptions underlying the basic fabric of monopoly capitalism and the structural inequality of American society.

Although society holds itself together by consensus or by constraint, it does so by providing the institutionalized means for special or single issue groups to realize their goals and objectives within the context of the agreed-upon legal system. Even though such groups seldom take the law into their own hands, there have been instances where they have consciously broken the law and have been willing to suffer the legal, physical, and psychological consequences in order to bring currency to their issue. Such groups have engaged in both violent and nonviolent behavior.

How does Conflict Theory I relate to community organizing? Although community organizations may be involved in multiple issues either serially or simultaneously, their focus is usually on immediate issues of policy change or survival, and less on organizing to facilitate basic structural changes. We will discuss more on community organizing later.

Conflict Theory II

Conflict Theory II, on the other hand, clearly breaks with the prevailing contemporary analysis of society by staking its claim to the historical fact that high power groups exploit low power groups. Although the state gives the appearance that it is value-free and neutral, it does play a significant role in the maintenance of social class dominance by supporting the owners of production and property. The state giving away our national heritage in the form of precious land, minerals, and natural resources at fire sale prices, or the state allowing special tax breaks, or the state passing laws that give elite groups an advantage over working class people, are examples of the state's partiality. Because of the exploitation of our national heritage and working people, they became key actors in the struggle to facilitate fundamental societal change; workers, in particular, became key actors for gaining control of production and the state apparatus for the equitable and just redistribution of our national resources. And while Conflict Theory I is more descriptive of social class, Conflict

Theory II is more dynamic and revolutionary.

In addition, Conflict Theory II scholar-activists feel that amassing small truths from specialized knowledge can never yield the larger, more significant truths about the social order itself. Conflict Theory I theorists complicate class struggle with descriptive data to a point where any meaningful action is muted.

Within the urban context, a small number of Conflict Theory II groups are working in unions to organize labor against owners of production. There have also been vocal Marxist groups on college campuses who espouse the rhetoric of fundamental societal change.

Although we make the distinction between Conflict Theories I and II for conceptual reasons, such differences are not always the case. There are community and scholar-activists with a Conflict Theory II perspective who work in community organizations with a Conflict Theory I perspective. The assumption is that an organizer should start where the people are ideologically, and, as the struggle for social and economic justice intensifies, this may lead people to a Conflict Theory II perspective. Such organizers may see conflict on a continuum, rather than as two distinct ideological positions.

Critique of Conflict Theories I and II

The pluralist special interest paradigm makes the assumption that individuals can make things right for themselves by finding collective expression through organization; they can make things right or seek justice for themselves by organizing and championing their self-interest. But the fact of is that there are some interest groups that have more power to champion their interests at the expense of other less powerful groups. Because of stark power differentials found within society, Conflict Theory I or interest group pluralism benefits the rich and the powerful more so than those in dire need. Now, let's critique Conflict Theory I with respect to the work of organizer Saul Alinsky.

While the Alinsky approach to organizing is effective in winning small victories to empower the poor and working class constituency, it has yet to improve significantly the condition of those it seeks to help. While this approach is rooted in Conflict Theory I, it fails to confront private ownership or the role of the state in capital accumulation, or to confront the fundamental contradictions found in society. Because Conflict Theory I scholar-activists have failed to develop a long-term strategy for the urban struggle, their micro approach to issues, without such a well defined ideology, may keep organizers from making the necessary connections between everyday actions and long-term viable solutions.

Yet, Conflict Theory II scholar-activists, although well-grounded in Marxist ideology, have failed in any meaningful way to win the hearts and minds of large numbers of people. During the 1960s and 1970s, people probably felt less need to support organizing activities for basic structural changes; they felt less need because of the notion of an expanding pie of affluence; they felt less need because, through institutionalized means, they could realize pecuniary goals and symbols of success. Yet, as the United States is losing its world hegemony and facing economic decline, moving us rapidly toward a two-tier society of the ''haves'' and ''have-nots," the working class and the poor might find more comfort in Conflict Theory II ideology.

Decline in U.S. World Hegemony

But what is giving rise to this decline in U.S. world hegemony and the U.S. economy? A number of progressive economists feel that the U.S. decline in world power began in the middle 1960s, when President Johnson tried to fight a war in Vietnam and declare a war on poverty at home without raising taxes. Organized labor used its ability to strike and bargain for higher wages, which cut into corporate profits. The Arab nations formed a cartel, not only to raise the price of oil, but to enable themselves to use their power in 1973 to implement an oil embargo, with devastating effect upon western economies. As American corporations closed plants and moved to distant shores in search of cheaper labor, they left local communities with lower tax bases, unemployed workers, and conditions of urban decay. In those instances where companies did not move to other parts of the world for a better deal on labor and resources, thousands of workers were replaced by computer driven machines. Corporate barons felt that the environmental movement, with its emphasis upon environmental regulations, gave them less flexibility to make profits. Liberation struggles were taking place in Africa and Central America, in spite of U.S. imperial might.

While recent U.S. administrations have attempted to reverse this perilous decline, it has cost working class people a considerable amount of hard earned money and security. In order to lower inflation and interest rates in an economy that was cascading out of control, the Federal Reserve planned and triggered the worst recession since the great depression, throwing thousands of people out of work. Also, federal monies were shifted from social programs to the Department of Defense; thousands of people were turned into the homeless, sleeping on city streets as the federal government used the age-old threat of communist expansionism to increase its military spending. This military spending came with a price that was placed on the backs of working class people, minorities, women, and the handicapped, and which increased the feminization of poverty.

As more of the working class moves from the manufac-turing to the service sector, they will make less money. While more will be employed as minimum wage earners, the avarice and greed of the middle and upper classes become more distinct through corporate mergers, and through white collar crime of the Wall Street variety. We are rapidly moving toward a two-tier society; and because the distribution of wealth is becoming so starkly imbalanced, it may move the masses from participating in a Conflict Theory I paradigm to a Conflict Theory II paradigm. Only time will tell.

Conflict Theory I: Reformist Strategies and the Environment

Conflict Theory I scholar-activists are knowledgeable about the bio-physical environment and acute in their calculations of cost benefit analysis and environmental decay, and such knowledge becomes the basis for lobbying public officials and participating in public hearings at the local, state, and national levels. It becomes the basis for organizing their campaigns against corporations who violate environmental laws. They have also protested unsafe conditions of toxic dumpsites, highway construction that takes prime farmland out of production, and the building of nuclear power plants.

Although many of them protest the harmful effects to the environment, others champion appropriate technology, voluntary simplicity, and bio-regionalism. While these ideas become the solutions to our environmental problems, the emphasis is upon the ''technological fix'' or individual choice--not basic changes in political or economic structures.

Conflict Theory II: Radical Environmental Strategies

Where reformers seek to control pollution of various kinds through laws and the ''technological fix,'' radicals call for a total reconstruction of the political economy. Their orientation is macro in character in that they not only critique Western industrial society, with all its shortcomings, but they make a compelling international critique as well. While their Third World perspective links the lion's share of resource utilization and depletion to Western imperialism and structural dependency that systematically exploit and deplete the resources of underdeveloped countries, they also observe the incompatibility of an ever-expanding industrial society and the preservation of environmental quality. This forces them to organize grassroots people and labor against capitalism wherever it prevails.

They see little meaning in separating environmental problems from the corporate state, and they are compelled to observe the total picture. They believe that corporations and the state must be controlled by workers in order for them to be more responsive to the people. Through advocacy and support, public planning becomes an institutionalized means for addressing the inequality issue and providing protection against resource depletion and environmental degradation. Only through this process can any chances of social and economic justice be rendered.

Our world view, historically rooted in Western thought, perceiving ourselves as a distinct species from our surroundings, and perceiving the world as a place to be manipulated at will to satisfy our own ends regardless of environmental consequences, can no longer be tolerated. It is painfully clear that the exponential use of our biological capital will undermine our basic institutions and poison our surroundings, threatening our health and, in fact, our very survival here on this planet earth. We have to create a new social and environmental paradigm, one that is not anthropocentric in character, but rather one that considers all living things on a continuum and takes into account sound social and ecological planning and conservation.

Because the problems of environmental and social decay are so enormous, they place a tremendous burden upon environmental advocates. To organize along the Conflict Theory II paradigm is definitely a Herculean task. It must include organizing progressive state and national legislators, middle and working class people, environmentalists, and farmers into a coalition to change our world view, our cultural and economic habits--to make them more supportive of a sustainable social and environmental future. We have to forge a coalition that will address the issues of exponential growth, nationalism, military waste, and technologies of death, and replace these with a world community where people's needs are met within a sustainable and healthy environment. We have to create a society that is more participatory, that gives more meaning to people's lives, and that allows people to reach their highest potential without blatant disregard of other living things. This is the challenge for year 2000 and beyond. It must be done, or we will surely perish.

Questions:

Return to the pages where the buttons are located. Pick two more---one you agree with, and one you do not agree with. What does your choice of buttons say about conflict? What does your button say about Conflict Theory I and Conflict Theory II? What does your choice of buttons say about you with respect to Conflict Theories I and II?

What about your friends and family? Where do you think they would place themselves with respect to Conflict Theories I and II?

What is a realistic coalition for social and environmental change for the future?

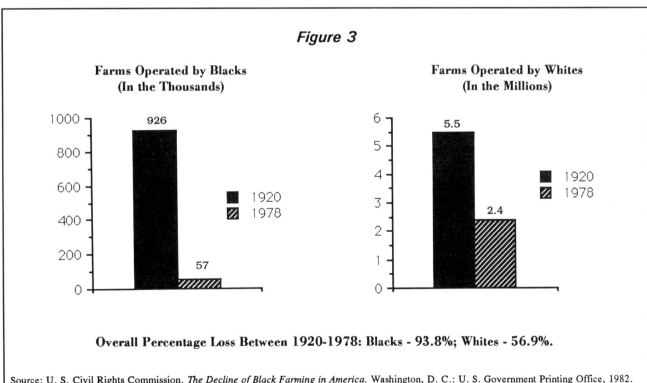

Figure 3

**Farms Operated by Blacks
(In the Thousands)**

926 — 1920
57 — 1978

**Farms Operated by Whites
(In the Millions)**

5.5 — 1920
2.4 — 1978

Overall Percentage Loss Between 1920-1978: Blacks - 93.8%; Whites - 56.9%.

Source: U. S. Civil Rights Commission. *The Decline of Black Farming in America.* Washington, D. C.: U. S. Government Printing Office, 1982.

Session Number Three: Using Conflict

Objectives of Session

To provide opportunities for you to engage in value clarification with respect to conflict and the unequal distribution of power in America.

To learn more about conflict theory.

Design Flow in Minutes

5 minutes Agenda review.
10 minutes Excitement sharing.
45 minutes Continue questionnaire discussion in groups of three.
10 minutes Break.
35 minutes Pick two other buttons--one you agree with and one you do not agree with; discuss the three questions at the end of *Concept Paper II on Action Research* in the groups of three.
20 minutes Evaluation and summary.

Homework

After having learned about Conflict Theories I and II, we now return to developing skills for doing action research. Following is a list of ways of finding information about any corporation that has been derelict in its social and environmental responsibilities. After studying the list, add to it in the blank spaces provided.

Then read the telephone scenario which follows, and be prepared to discuss the questions at the end of it. Next read the descriptions of corporations, and select a first and second choice to research. Finally, read the paper entitled *Action Research and Financial Reports.*

Ways to Find Information about Corporations

Questionnaires
Door knocking
Checking personal vitas
License plate numbers
Articles of incorporation
Corporate income tax statements
Current and former political opponents
Inside corporate contacts
Interview former employees
Company publications
Trade publications
New York Times Index
Soil sampling activities and reports
Water sampling activities and reports
Environmental Impact Statements
Interview union members
Building permits
Interview secretaries and former secretaries
Interview current and former janitors
Court records
Cancelled checks

On the lines below, list or brainstorm other ways of finding or retrieving information about corporations:

_____

_____

_____

_____

_____

_____

_____

_____

_____

_____

Telephone Scenario

In order to do action research, it takes lots of persistence. You cannot take no for an answer. Often, the resistance is in proportion to the importance of the information wanted. Don't be discouraged, and ask for information in a way that shows sincerity and confidence. Below is a telephone scenario adapted from *Company Information: A Model Investigation* by W. Law-Yone and D. M. Jablonski (Washington, DC: Washington Researchers, 1980). It demonstrates a hassle factor of nine on a scale of ten, with ten being high. The researcher is in the process of finding information on Perdue Farms, an agribusiness chicken-processing company. The researcher has made several telephone calls to various people in the Library of Congress. The library puts out a bibliographic series called *Tracer Bullets,* which contains important information on corporate business, directing the reader to various publications on scientific data and technical topics. The researcher calls the Library of Congress to get such information, and here is what follows:

The first voice answered, a Mr. Liao; he gave me another number to call. "This is just the reading room," he explained.

For purposes of the detailed log I was keeping through each step of my study, I asked him what the number he had just given me was for.

"That's the reference section," he said.

"Then what is this I'm reaching?"

Then, inexplicably, Mr. Liao wanted to know if I lived in Washington. I told him that I did. "Thank you," he said and hung up.

Reflecting on the mysterious ways of the librarian, I called the number he had given me and repeated my question about poultry and Tracer Bullets. The second voice informed me that all questions on agriculture were answered by Mr. Liao. He then gave me the first number I had dialed. "But I just talked to Mr. Liao," I said, "and he told me to call here."

"Please hold a minute." I could hear a muffled voice consulting with someone, possibly Mr. Liao. The voice returned to the telephone and announced that "all such inquiries must be directed to..." (and gave me a third number).

Voice #3 listened to my request—and told me to call #1. Like the patient researcher I had resolved to be, I explained that I had done so, and that #1 had steered me to #2, who in turn had led me here.

"They told you to call here?" said #3, sounding non-plussed. "This is the reference section of the main reading room."

(I had an image of three men sitting in an alcove of the Library of Congress, each with a telephone in front of him, playing a game of musical phones. The object of the game was to refer each caller to the next person. The one stuck with the call when the music stopped was the loser.)

I heard voice #3 saying, "There must be someone there who doesn't know what he has. Hold on and I'll try to call that extension."

Number 3 then returned to me. "That extension is busy," he said, "Try calling them again and tell them they have the Tracer Bullets."

My impulse was to dial one of those numbers and demand: "Okay, who has the Bullets on the pullets?"

Instead I dialed #1. This time a female voice answered. I almost said, "Could you connect me with the musical phones?" Once more, I recited my inquiry about Tracer Bullets and the poultry industry.

"Let me check," she said, and disappeared.

Number 2 came back on next.

"Can I help you?"

"About the chickens," I said, "Do you have any Tracer Bullets?"

"We have nothing here on marketing," explained #2.

I had said nothing about marketing—but I was determined to keep my head. "Do you have any Tracer Bul-

lets?" I persisted.

"Call this number," replied #2, giving me #3 again.

"Do you have any Tracer Bullets?"

"No, I mean, yes, we do have Tracer Bullets," said #2 at last, "but nothing on the poultry industry. Hold on, please."

At that point, a new female voice came on. "Can I help you?"

I recounted for her my recent hardships.

"Hang on for a second," she said. I had given up hope by the time she returned a few minutes later—with an answer that exceeded all expectations.

"The poultry industry," she said, "is a good heading in our terminal. There are 56 books catalogued since 1968. Come into our main building and ask to see our LCCC file and BIBL file. Look up Poultry Industry. Then look at the books in the HDs, and the periodicals in the HS. Afterwards, go across the street to the Thomas Jefferson Building and look at the S books on agriculture. Lastly, ask to see the NRCM file. You should have a fairly good start by then."

Have you had an experience like the above? If so, under what circumstances? What other strategies could the researcher have used on the phone? Can you persist this long to get information? Are you good about speaking up to authority and getting what you want?

Corporations To Be Researched

Below are corporations to be researched. The list is by no means inclusive. If you are interested in researching a corporation not listed, then simply pick it instead of those listed here. It is better to work in small groups of six, so you can be supportive of one another while doing research. Sometimes research is rather tedious and boring—but it doesn't have to be. Take a few minutes to study the corporations listed below, picking one based upon the brief description offered. Don't let the names intimidate you.

International Paper

Incorporated in New York, 1941. Primarily U.S. and Canadian based. Produces pulp, paper, paper packaging, and wood products. Through the company's subsidiary, GCO Minerals, they explore for and develop minerals and plants. They also harvest rice in the Southwest.

Georgia-Pacific

Incorporated in Georgia, 1927. Multi-national corporation. Produces building products, pulp, paper, and chemical products. Owns timber and mineral lands that supply raw materials for its own industries. GP owns 416 million acres and controls 515,000 acres of land in Canada and the U.S. It also controls 2.6 million acres in Brazil and Indonesia.

Eli Lilly Company

Incorporated in Indiana, 1901. Facilities in U.S., Puerto Rico, and 34 other countries. It is a multi-national corporation with a long list of subsidiaries. Involved in discovery, development, and sales of drugs and other chemical compounds for human health, agricultural, and cosmetic products.

International Business Machines

Incorporated in New York, 1911. Produces worldwide information systems, equipment, and services; data processing, telecommunications, office systems, copiers, education, and testing materials. Serves the space, science, education, government, defense, and business sectors.

- International Telephone and Telegraph

Incorporated in Delaware in 1968, succeeding a company of the same name that was incorporated in Maryland in 1920. Multi-national corporation with a huge list of subsidiaries. Activities include sales, research and development in telecommunications and electronics systems, industrial and automotive products, insurance (Casualty and Life Insurance Co.), and timber, mining, and coal resources.

American Telephone and Telegraph ("Ma Bell")

Incorporated in New York, 1885. Telephone communications systems throughout continental U.S. Of interest: recent sales of smaller telephone subsidiaries to enable it to diversify.

Dow Chemical Company

Incorporated in Delaware, 1947. Multi-national corporation with huge listing of subsidiaries. Produces wide variety of products from organic/inorganic chemicals to plastics. Of interest: local plant in Midland, Michigan.

Alcoa

Incorporated as the Rainbow Production Corporation in Ohio, 1952. Corporation with large listing of primarily U.S. subsidiaries. Diversified corporation involved in paper and metal products, food service equipment, containers and glassware, automotive products, as well as the chemical, rubber, and plastics industries. Also through their subsidiaries (Barnes and Tucker Co. and Upshur Coal Corporation), coal mining in central Pennsylvania and northern West Virginia.

General Electric

Incorporated in New York in 1892. Diversified corporation with focus on systems for generation, transmission, and distribution of electricity. Produces major houseware appliances, lighting, audio, and cablevision products. Involved in natural resource mining of coal, coke (in Australia), uranium, copper, iron, oil, and natural gas production.

U.S. Steel

Incorporated in Delaware, 1965; predecessor company incorporated in 1901 in New Jersey. U.S. based corporation with many subsidiaries, including mining and mineral exploration in South Africa. Focus on steel, chemicals, and resource development. Involved in fabricating and engineering, domestic transport, and utility subsidiaries.

McDermot

Incorporated in Delaware, 1946. Involved in marine construction services (i.e., offshore rigs and pipelines), and power generation systems and equipment (including nuclear fuel assemblies and engineering materials).

Allied

Diversified corporation with holdings primarily in U.S., Canada, and Europe. Involved in oil and gas production, chemicals, fiber, plastics, and electronic products. Of interest: acquisition of Bendix Corporation.

Exxon

Incorporated in New Jersey, 1882. Largest multi-national corporation in terms of revenue (1981). Operates in U.S. and nearly 100 other countries. Involved in exploration for production of crude oil, natural gas, and petroleum products. Also exploration/mining/sale of coal and uranium, and fabrication of nuclear fuel.

Tenneco

Incorporated in Delaware, 1954. Multi-national involved in diverse lines: oil exploration and production, processing and marketing of oil and chemicals, shipbuilding, life insurance, fibers, agricultural products, construction and farm equipment, and natural gas pipelines.

Action Research on Financial Reports

If you have had a course in accounting, then you don't need to be told the basics to understand what's presented in annual reports. If you haven't had courses in accounting and find reading financial reports "over your head," then consult *How to Read a Financial Report*. This booklet will not make you an expert on financial reports, but it will give you a working understanding of them. Remember, many investigative reporters or action researchers are not experts at the beginning of an investigative or research endeavor, but they may be when the task is completed.

Therefore, if you have a problem with a company's financial statement, then figure out what resources you have. Do you have a friend or a relative who is an accountant? What about your roommate or some business student or some business faculty member? Remember, this kind of work will undoubtedly take you to many different experts. Don't be discouraged. Be assertive about what you want and go after it. Remember the *Ten Theses on Power Structure Research.*

Most annual reports are displayed in three different ways, namely: 1) pictures, 2) prose, and 3) figures. On the whole, the prose is usually straightforward and quite understandable, while pictures are useful in making the presentation both clearer and more interesting. The income statement and balance sheet are the hardest for the average person to comprehend in any meaningful way. Basically, the income statement tells how the company did this year compared to last year, whether it had a good or bad year in profits, and to what extent. The balance sheet tells how strong its finances are by showing what the company owns on a certain date. And don't forget the footnotes. Although small and hard to read at times, they are nevertheless important, and a considerable amount of information can be gleaned from them.

Financial reports should not be overrated. The information obtained from them can be useful in different ways--in determining to what degree a company can afford plant improvements or improvement of working conditions for its employees, or, as mentioned before, gains and losses in profits or the rate of profit investors are getting from their stock. But companies have a way of juggling numbers to suit their own needs. Further, the balance sheet and income statements are like still pictures, only capturing the corporation at a point in time. The reality of corporations is more like a moving picture, constantly changing, each frame giving a different picture. Even though the financial report may hide a lot of things from us or only capture the corporation at a given time, or yield a small amount of information compared to other reference materials, it is nonetheless important to know some ac-

counting concepts.

Because many companies juggle financial statements to their own end, these statements become political documents. This is not to say that they are engaged in illegal activities; manipulation of financial statements is quite legitimate, making companies look "good" or "bad," depending upon the company's aim. Therefore, it is important to keep in mind the political character of these reports. Don't let the business library intimidate you. There are thousands of business references in the library, with an abundance of information to be consumed by the researcher. Researchers don't have to be financial wizards to understand much of the information written about corporations. You can definitely learn a lot through nontechnical information. The 10K forms are an important information source. Ask the reference person how to gain access to them. In addition, if you find a new reference in the library that is helpful, pass it on, and let other researchers know about it.

By working from this manual, you are getting more help and support than action researchers normally do in the field. They do not have someone to guide them around, putting them in touch with references. You will have to learn to be creative, assertive, hard-working, and persistent to retrieve the information you want. Remember, the information is there, or someone knows the answer. It's a question of how to get it.

There is no strict methodological way of doing action research. It is based upon skill, hunches, creativity, commitment, perseverance, and motivation. In the pages of this manual, an attempt is made to give some general outlines for gathering information on corporations and governmental agencies. These suggestions are by no means all-inclusive or conclusive. Before getting started, try to find general information about the corporation by looking up concepts that are not understandable in a dictionary or encyclopedia. In fact, you may want to make a glossary of terms to refer to as your research continues.

Trade associations are sources of a considerable amount of information on corporations. Consult them early in your efforts to learn about current issues and concerns; interview someone from one of the trade associations if possible. Often, they can be helpful in sharpening the focus of your research.

On the following pages are lists of popular references on business which can be found in most public libraries. Glance through this list to get an idea of the variety of resources available to you. Take the list to the library and update it as you find additional resources.

Business Resources in the Public Library

American Register of Exporters and Importers
New York, NY 10038
(212) 227-4030

Business Information Source
University of California Press
2223 Fulton St., Berkeley, CA 94720
(415) 642-6682

Business Periodicals Index
H. W. Wilson Company
950 University Ave., Bronx, NY 10452
(212) 588-8400

Congressional Information Service Index
Congressional Information Services, Inc.
Washington, DC 20014
(202) 654-1550

*Directory of American Firms Operating
    in Foreign Countries*
World Trade Academic Press, Inc.
50E. 42nd St., New York, NY 10017
(212) 697-4999

Directory of Corporate Affiliations
National Register Publishing, Co.
5201 Old Orchard Rd., Skokie, IL 60076
(312) 966-8500

Directory Information Service
Gale Research Company
Book Tower, Detroit, MI 48226
(313) 961-2242

Dun & Bradstreet Middle Market Directory
Dun & Bradstreet Million Dollar Directory
Dun & Bradstreet Principal International Business
Dun & Bradstreet Reference Book
Dun & Bradtreet, Inc.
99 Church St., New York, NY 10007
(212) 285-7376

The Encyclopedia of Associations
Gale Research Company
Book Tower, Detroit, MI 48226
(313) 961-2242

F&S Index of Corporations and Industries
F&S Index International
F&S Index Europe
Predicasts, Inc.
11001 Cedar Ave., Cleveland, OH 44106
(216) 795-3000

Guide to American Directories
B. Klein Publications
P. O. Box 8503, Coral Springs, FL 33065
(305) 227-4030

Kelly's Manufacturers and Merchants Directory
Kelly's Directories, Ltd.
Neville House Eden St., Kingston upon Thames,
    Surrey, KT1 1BY, England
01-546-7722

Moody's Bank and Financial Manual
Moody's Industrial Manual
Moody's Investors Service, Inc.
99 Church St., New York, NY 10007
(212) 553-0300

Standard Directory of Advertisers
National Register Publishing Company, Inc.
20 E. 46th St., Room 603, New York, NY 10017
(212) 682-0677

Standard & Poor's Corporation Discriptions
*Standard & Poor's Register of Corporations, Directors,
    and Executives*
Standard and Poor's
345 Hudson St., New York, NY 10014
(212) 925-6400, Ext. 303

Tax Form 8 K
Tax Form 10 K

Thomas Register of American Manufacturers
Thomas Publishing Company
1 Pennsylvania Plaza, New York, NY 10001
(212) 695-0500

Business Resources in the Public Library (continued)

Trade Names Directory
Gale Research Company
Book Tower, Detroit, MI 48226
(313) 961-2242

U. S. Industrial Directory
Cahners Publishing Company
1200 Summer St., Stamford, CT 06905
(203) 327-2450

Wall Street Journal Index
Dow Jones Books
P. O. Box 455, Chicopee, MA 01021
(413) 592-7761

Who Owns Whom
O. W. Roskill & Company, Ltd.
Dun & Bradstreet International, Ltd.
P. O. Box 3224, Chuurch Street Station,
  New York, NY 10008

Figure 4

Restoring Tax Justice

Distribution of the impact by income size group of proposed increased taxes on the wewalthy. Nearly three-quarters of the burden will fall upon those who make $200,000 or more a year.

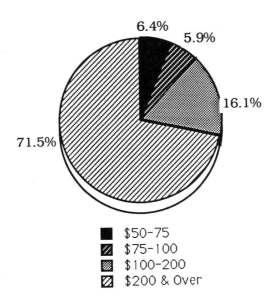

6.4%
5.9%
16.1%
71.5%

■ $50-75
▨ $75-100
▦ $100-200
▨ $200 & Over

Income Range (in thousands of dollars)

Source: Jackson, J. *Paying for Our Dreams: A Budget Plan for Jobs, Peace, and Justice.* (Unpublished, 1988).

Session Number Four: Implementing Action Research

Objectives of the Session

To provide opportunities to: 1) Share action research and telephone scenario strategies; and 2) to select a corporation for implementing action research.

Design Flow in Minutes

5 minutes   Agenda review.
20 minutes Discuss creative ways of retrieving information.
15 minutes Share information in total group.
10 minutes Break.
20 minutes Discuss telephone scenario. The questions at the end of the scenario are to serve as the basis for discussion.
20 minutes Organize yourselves into groups of four to six to select a corporation for implementing action research.
15 minutes Summary and evaluation.

Homework

Using the references found in the business section of any good public library, as listed on the previous two pages, begin researching the corporation you have selected. These references give you considerable information on corporate activities of both a technical and non-technical nature. Become familiar with these references; they are important for finding information on corporations. Specific questions for homework are as follows:

1. What is the history of the organization, of its original owners, charter, goals, products, and mergers? When was it founded?

2. What is the size and scope of the organization--plant and facility locations, products and production processes, divisions, subsidiaries, affiliates, subcontractors, raw materials needs, and sources of markets for products?

After answering these questions, read the following three problem sets entitled *All the President's Men*, *Ben Chemical Company,* and *Kerr-McGee*.

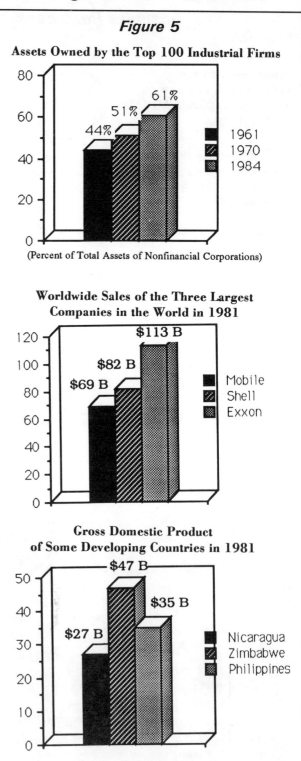

Figure 5

Assets Owned by the Top 100 Industrial Firms

(Percent of Total Assets of Nonfinancial Corporations)

1961
1970
1984

Worldwide Sales of the Three Largest Companies in the World in 1981

Mobile
Shell
Exxon

Gross Domestic Product of Some Developing Countries in 1981

Nicaragua
Zimbabwe
Philippines

Source: Foreword from: Folbre, N. *A Field Guide to the U.S. Economy.* N.Y.: Pantheon Books, 1987. Center for Popular Economics.

Three Problem Sets

Problem Set 1:
All The President's Men

In *All the President's Men,* Woodward and Bernstein reported using a subtle and convincing method of demonstrating their commitment to confidentiality when they began interviewing employees of the Committee for the Re-Election of the President (CREEP) in the summer of 1972 to gather information for what turned out to be their prize-winning expose. In their late-night appearances at homes of CREEP employees, they would say "a friend at the committee (CREEP) told us you were disturbed by some of the things you saw going on there, that you would be a good person to talk to ... that you were absolutely straight and honest, and didn't know quite what to do." When the person they were seeking to interview asked which fellow employee had given the reporters the lead, Woodward and Bernstein politely, but firmly, refused to reveal the name of their source. They explained that their refusal was based on a commitment to confidential sources, giving an explicit assurance that the person's identity would be similarly protected. The other reason for not naming names, of course, was that the reporters were operating from an employee list smuggled out of the CREEP headquarters.

Their source at the committee was nonexistent; nevertheless, it was a door opener. By lying, Woodward and Bernstein probably shocked many people's ethical sensibilities. But, if Watergate hadn't been exposed, the corruption would have continued.

Reporters are often left in the position of attacking public officials for breaking one body of law--conflict of interest, for example--while having themselves broken other laws--stealing documents, perhaps--to prove conflict of interest.

Reporters sometimes find themselves in the position of breaking the law to gain the necessary information to expose a scandal or a conflict of interest. Should one break one set of laws in order to get at the law breakers? What do you think?

Problem Set 2:
Ben Chemical Company

Ben Chemical Company has been suspected of illegal dumping of waste in the Detroit area. The Michigan State Department of Natural Resources has received several calls about barrels of toxic waste that have been dumped along the side of the road. Just overnight, they appear. It's difficult to prove that the company is responsible for the dumping.

You work for a public interest group. It was agreed that you get a job at Ben Chemical as a secretary. After several weeks, you form a relationship with the office people so that you can inquire about the dumping processes. On several occasions you worked late, giving you a chance to look at records and checks written to a certain person for Thursday midnight runs. You suspect that this is the time when illegal dumping is taking place. You contact your organization to be on alert for Thursday midnight activities. Ben Chemical Company is then caught in the act. Your organization obtains pictures and other hard data.

What do you think about the situation? Should people misrepresent themselves in such an instance to gain information? What are other ways this information might have been obtained?

Problem Set 3: *Kerr-McGee*

You are married with one child and gainfully employed at Kerr-McGee Nuclear Corporation. You have just been elected to the local bargaining committee of the Oil, Chemical and Atomic Workers Union (OCAW). You know for a fact that Kerr-McGee was doctoring its fuel-rod quality-assurance records, leaving you unsure what faulty fuel rods might do in use. You read that nuclear scientists say defective rods need not be dangerous. If rods leak, they argue, the radiation inside them will just escape into the sodium solution that cools the reactor. If they continue to leak, the reactor will have to be shut down, radioactive water and steam will have to be drawn off somehow, to replace leaking rods--expensive, but not dangerous. Yet, you have also read that other nuclear scientists disagree. At best, they say, no one knows what would happen. Therefore, leaking fuel rods should be taken very seriously. At worst, they could cause a melt down. And you believe the latter.

Kerr-McGee does not know you have this information. You will be fired right on the spot if you bring this to negotiations. Meanwhile, a Kerr-McGee worker launched a drive to decertify the OCAW as the bargaining agent for all workers, union members or not. Thirty percent of the workers had signed a petition to this effect, indicating the union might be decertified. You really need this job at Kerr-McGee; it pays well. Treatment of your child's dyslexia (a serious reading problem) is very expensive. You are angry and you know that you will have to take some drastic action to make known the faulty fuel-rods. *What will that be?*

Session Number Five: Clarifying Values

Objective of the Session

To provide an opportunity to clarify your values on social and environmental change.

Design Flow in Minutes

5 minutes   Agenda review.
20 minutes Discuss problem sets: *All the President's Men, Ben Chemical Company,* and *Kerr-McGee.*
15 minutes Report on discussions.
5 minutes   Introduction to film.
50 minutes View *Looking at Sixty Minutes.*
A 15 minute discussion should follow on *Looking at Sixty Minutes.* An alternative would be to have the group divide into threes and have them take 20 minutes to design a role play for retrieving information. Groups have 30 minutes to act out their roles.

Homework

It is not only important for you to learn about action research and social and environmental conflict; it is equally important for you to confront your own personal values. Each person will have differing views on how information should be obtained and used. There are both institutional and non-institutinal prescribed means for obtaining data. It is up to you to determine the means of retrieving and using data.

Below are some questions to be answered about corporations. As a team you might want to divide up these questions. They are to be the basis for your team paper or report. (If this is used as an assignment for a class, then these questions as well as those on corporations in the previous lesson can be answered in the context of a written paper and/or an oral report.)

You may want to consult the financial definitions in the appendix of this manual.

1. What are the company's assets? What are its liabilities? What is its owner's equity?

2. Is the company financially sound? How satisfactory have its business activities been? How did you compute this?

3. What are its current assets? What are its fixed assets? What are its accounts receivable?

4. What was the corporation's net income (profits) last year?

5. How (to whom...in what form) were profits distrib-
uted? What was the difference between gross income and net income? What were its expenses?

6. What was the percentage of change in profits over the last 5 years?

7. What is the local U.S. impact of the company's investments in foreign countries? What is the short- and long-term effect? How does it affect self-determination? What is the effect on local politics and the economic health of local communities?

8. What are the litigations, anti-trust actions, consumer or environmental suits, acquisitions, and mergers? What are the research and development and advertising expenditures (in relation to, for example, pollution control or employee benefits)? What are the domestic and international development of new markets and natural and human resources? What are the attitudes among employees toward management and company policies, such as health plans and safety conditions? What are the communty and race relations like?

9. Pick one of the directors of the corporation and research his or her background. Useful resources to research VIPs are listed on the next page.

10. What is the impact of the company's investment in foreign countries? What is the effect upon self-determination, distribution of wealth, wages, jobs, and environmental dangers? What is the company's connection with other American governmental agencies? What are the tax shelters, trade agreements, and products sold by the company? What are the resources it needs or uses? How do foreign profits compare with U.S. profits?

12. Read information on state, local, and private sources which follows under the heading "Action Research: State Government." List information you might need from these levels of government.

13. Addresses and telephone numbers for state agenies in Michigan are presented in the manual as examples; take a local phone book for your state or area and track down addresses and phone numbers of similar resources in your state. A two-page set of forms is provided as guidance in this effort, as well as a sample page of potential local and private sources. You can develop your own forms and tables for such information.

Resources about Personalities and Elites

Following are reference sources on personalities and elites which you can find in most public libraries. These sources can be used to gather information on leaders of the corporations you are researching. The sources are arranged in categories for ease of use.

General Biographical Sources
Who's Who in the East
Who's Who in the Midwest
Who's Who in the South and Southwest
Who's Who in the West
Who's Who in Oregon and the Western States
World Biography
Outstanding Young Men of America
Current Biography
Biography Index
Social Register

Lawyers
Who's Who in Law
Martindale-Hubell Law Directory
Directory of American Judges
The Lawyer's Directory
The American Bar Association Directory
Eminent Judges and Lawyers of the American Bar
Eminent Judges and Lawyers of the Northwest

Foundation Officers and Trustees
Foundation Directory

Local Power Elites
Polk's City Directory

Business People and Financiers
Moody's Banking and Finance
Moody's Industrials
Moody's Utilities
Moody's Transports
Million Dollar Directory
Middle Market Directory
Directory of Shopping Centers International
Who's Who in Commerce and Industry
Who's Who in Banking
Rand McNally's International
Banker's Register
Who's Who in Advertising
Who's Who in Public Relations
Who's Who in Publishing
Who's Who in Aviation and Astronautics
Who's Who in Engineering
Shipping World Yearbook

Political Leaders and Government Officials
American Politics
Congressional Directory
Biographical Dictionary of the American Congress
International Yearbook and Statesmen's Who's Who
Who's Who in the Nation's Capitol
Directory of American Judges
The Almanac of American Politics

People in Cultural Fields
American Men of Science
Directory of American Scholars
Leaders in American Science
Who's Who in American Art
Who's Who in American Education
*Presidents and Deans of American Colleges and
    Universities*
American Men of Medicine
Rockefeller Foundation Directory of Fellowship Awards

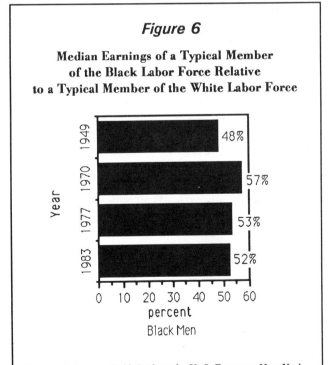

Figure 6

**Median Earnings of a Typical Member
of the Black Labor Force Relative
to a Typical Member of the White Labor Force**

Source: Folbre, N. *Field Guide to the U. S. Economy.* New York: Pantheon Books, 1987.

Implementing Action Research at the State and Local Levels

Considerable amounts of valuable information on corporations are found in places other than public libraries. This is particularly true for information on small, local companies. State, county, and local governments can often provide the necessary information. Every organization doing business within a state must file a voluminous amount of paperwork with government offices, including financial statements, stock prospectuses, and reports of inspections and investigations of businesses or buildings. Additionally, most states have laws mandating that state officials make virtually all documents open to the public.

This does not mean that you can turn state officials into your very own private researchers. They have too many other responsibilities. Forming a personal relationship with them, however, can prove to be helpful, particularly if you can meet with them face-to-face. In fact, some forms of information are made available only if you visit the appropriate governmental office. Other information can be mailed to you directly. In addition, the state can charge fees for duplication and time spent searching records.

As mentioned on the previous page, state agencies on the list that follows are only for Michigan. Parallel agencies will be found in other states. Take time and consult your phone directory for addresses and phone numbers of agencies in your state. Write or call them for available information. Once this information has been compiled and listed in your manual, scan the list for appropriate agencies for further information.

When you find the office you want, contact it by mail, telephone, or in person. Be specific about what you want, remembering there is some information that is strictly confidential and difficult to obtain. But most of what you want will be available. It is helpful to refer to documents by name. Again, do not hesitate to ask for help in finding information.

A key source for information on agencies in your state may be *How to Find Information about Companies*, edited by D. Jablonsky, and published in 1979 by Washington Researchers, 918 16th St., N.W., Washington, D.C. 20006.

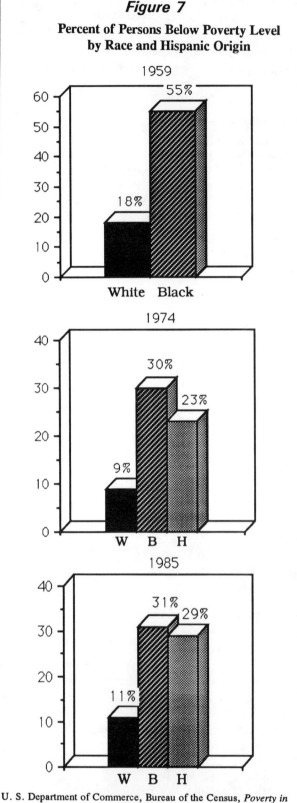

Figure 7

Percent of Persons Below Poverty Level by Race and Hispanic Origin

U. S. Department of Commerce, Bureau of the Census, *Poverty in the United States 1985*. (Washington D.C.: U. S. Government Printing Office, 1987).

Michigan State Agencies

Air Pollution
Air Quality Division, Department of Natural Resources
P. O. Box 30028, Lansing, MI 48909
(517) 322-1336

Banking
Bank and Trust Division, Financial Institutions Bureau,
    Department of Commerce
P. O. Box 30224, Law Building, Lansing, MI 48909
(517) 373-6950

Commerce
Corporation and Securities Bureau, Dept. of Commerce
P. O. Box 30054, Lansing, MI 48909
(517) 373-0493

Consumer Protection
Consumer Protection Complaints and Enforcement
Office of the Attorney General
525 W. Ottawa St., Law Bldg., Lansing, MI 48909
(517) 373-1140

Economic Development
Office of Economic Development, Dept. of Commerce
P. O. Box 30225, Lansing, MI 48909
(517) 373-8312

Environment
Bureau of Environment and Occupational Health,
    Department of Public Health
P. O. Box 30035, 3500 N. Logan St., Lansing, MI 48909
(517) 373-1410

Food and Drugs
Drugs
Dept. of Licensing and Regulation, Board of Pharmacy
P. O. Box 30018, 905 Southland Ave., Lansing, MI 48909
(517) 373-0620
Food
Food Inspection Div., Dept. of Agriculture
P. O. Box 30017, Lansing, MI 48909
(517) 373-1060

Franchise
Corporations and Securities Bureau, Dept. of Commerce
P. O. Box 30222, 6546 Mercantile Way, Lansing, MI
    48909
(517) 373-0485

Insurance
Insurance Bureau, Dept. of Commerce
P. O. Box 30220, 1048 Pierpont Bldg., Lansing, MI
    48909
(517) 373-0220

Labor
Department of Labor
309 N. Washington, Lansing, MI 48909
(517) 373-9600

Occupational and Professional Licensing
Department of Licensing and Regulation
P. O. Box 30018, Lansing, MI 48909
(517) 373-1870

Occupational Safety and Health
Bureau of Safety and Regulation, Dept. of Labor
P. O. Box 30015, 7150 Harris Dr., Lansing, MI 48909
(517) 322-1814

Purchasing
Purchasing Dept., Dept. of Management and Budget
Mason Bldg., 2nd Floor, Lansing, MI 48909
(517) 373-0300

Securities
Corporations and Securities, Dept. of Commerce
P. O. Box 30222, 6546 Mercantile Way, Lansing, MI
    48909
(517) 373-0485

Uniform Commercial Code
Uniform Commercial Code Division, Secretary of State
Lansing, MI 48918
(517) 373-0810

Water Pollution
Water Quality Division, Dept. of Natural Resources
P. O. Box 30028, Lansing, MI 48909
(517) 373-1947

Form for Addresses and Telephone Numbers of Agencies in Your State

Air Pollution

Banking

Commerce

Consumer Protection

Economic Development

Environment

Food and Drugs

Franchise

Insurance

Labor

Occupational and Professional Licensing

Occupational Safety and Health

Purchasing

Securities

Uniform Commercial Code

Water Pollution

Local resources

Source	Document	Association
Property or tax assessor	Records or cards listing the value of property and tax assessment. They list the owner of properties, describe buildings on property, and tell the size of the tract. A sketch or photo might be attached. They show assessed value of the land buildings. Sometimes the market value is given. Also tax maps, plats, aerial photos, and surveys may be helpful to locate a parcel to determine what's on it. Ask staff members to help you find documents. Ask questions if you don't understand the documents. Note that assesed values seldom equal market values, but they can be easily computed. Information on cards may be dated.	International Association of Assessment Officers 1313 W. 60th St. Chicago, Il. 60637
Planning Department	This is the place were developers submit papers for permits. Such information at the planning office may be simple or complex, including environmental impact statements. The filings sometimes describe bonds posted and demonstrations of financial ability (loan guarantees, etc.). There are also regional and special district planning bodies in some areas. Ask planning staff for help in getting what you want.	Nat.. Association of Counties 1735 New York Ave. N.W. Washington, D.C. 2006
County City Clerk's Office (Recorder or Register of Deeds)	Investigate the grantor and grantee indexes. You need to know the difference between the two. They list a description of the parcel, including its size and legal description--sometimes the mortgage payment. State tax stamps affixed to the deeds may be used to estimate the parcel's purchase price. Maps and plats can be used to help locate land.	
Chamber of Commerce	Often they have a "Better Business Bureau" to monitor business practices of member organizations. They handle complaints against them. The Chamber is usually familiar with business activities, including firms seeking to locate in the community. They sometimes compile economic surveys on a given area.	
The Local Newspaper	Newspapers have library files that are sometimes open to the public. They are good for finding background information about companies or individuals. Business editors and writers are additional sources familiar with economic and business trends, including large land transactions and company acquisitions.	

*Information on local sources and private sources came from : Jablonski, D. (ed.) **How to Find Information about Companies.** Washington, D.C.: Washington Researchers, 1979 (918 16th St., N.W. 20006, (202 828-4800)).

Session Number Six: Retrieving Information

Objectives of the Session

To share action research information within teams.

To provide opportunities for you to explore other avenues for retrieving information.

Design Flow in Minutes

5 minutes Agenda review.
10 minutes Excitement sharing.
45 minutes Teams to share information within teams.
10 minutes Break.
20 minutes Review resources at the state and local levels, as well as private resources.
15 minutes Force field analysis.
10 minutes Evaluation.

Homework

As a team, do a force field analysis. Pick something specific you want to change about the corporation being researched. Spend a considerable amount of time thinking this through before undertaking a force field analysis.

As a team, design a timeline, based on information from your force field analysis. This is to be done in teams.

The following additional information on action research and explanation of force field analysis will assist you in these efforts.

More on Action Research

Remember, the library is not the only place to obtain information. Information can be obtained from government agencies, questionnaires, personal interviews, court records, and the like. Researchers may want to review sources of information from the list brainstormed previously. In retrieving information, look for conflicts of interest, and inconsistencies in documents or stories. For instance, in the coal miner's strike in Harlan County, the judge who presided over the case was also found to be a coal company owner. When this information was brought to his attention, he had to dismiss himself from the trial because of conflict of interest. If the state procurement office is purchasing only Chevrolets, is there some kind of kickback taking place? If public officials are being researched, one of the most immediate ways to obtain information is by interviewing the people they ran against in the last election. If interested in corporate information, try to find whistle-blowers or potential ones.

The information obtained from library sources is overwhelming. Don't panic if the information is not under-standable. Be persistent in asking questions of people who might know the answers. Researchers should make it a point to write down new information, filing it away so that it can be easily retrieved. Three by five index cards with cross-references can be organized for easy access to information. Action researchers are not expected to know all the answers, but they are expected to learn enough to plan an effective strategy for social change.

The action researcher needs to think about using the information: What goals and objectives are feasible ones? Who or what information will be appropriate in reaching stated goals and objectives? What or who is the target of your change effort? Who or what department within government or industry is the antagonist? But before proceeding with a strategy, check each fact at least three times with outside sources. Nothing can blow your credibility more than to have inaccurate information.

There are a number of strategies and tactics used to facilitate Social and Environmental Change (SEC) such as: 1) Divesting and reinvesting money in companies with environmentally sound programs; 2) Boycotting companies that pollute and destroy your surroundings. These are only two examples of activities to bring about pressure on corporations to be more responsible to the biophysical environment. There are other strategies such as lobbying, direct-action nonviolence, guerilla theater, teach-ins, and a variety of media strategies (for more information see the "Tactics and Skills Chart" in the appendix of this manual). Strategies are often more effective if used in combination with other strategies, such as using the media to help widen the arena of conflict, thus bringing visibility to the organization or the issue.

Strategies

The remaining sections of this manual will deal with strategies. Reflect on a corporation under investigation or one that poses an environmental problem to the community. Think of a specific problem to solve. What specific action could the corporation take to alleviate the problem (specific goal[s])? Think of all the driving forces in favor of change. Think of all the hindering forces maintaining the status quo. Think of resources needed to increase the strength of the driving force. This is called a force field analysis. The force field charts on the following pages are used to help generate strategies for social change.

Force Field Analysis

Thus far we have been discussing the impact of corporate power upon the environment and upon ourselves. What we want to do now is to pressure corporations to be more responsible to our surroundings.

The following exercise is an attempt to help us do just that. It is called a force field analysis, a concept developed by Kurt Lewin, a psychologist. Wherever there is a force moving in one direction, there is usually a counter-force. When forces are equal on both sides of the vertical line in the field, this represent the status quo. We need to recognize the variety of forces that exist and mobilize them to assist us in moving in a given direction. This would result in SEC.

The action researcher has to be rather specific in stating the problem and fairly specific in stating goals. Now, out of all the information you have accumulated on your corporation, pick a specific problem to work on, one that can be realistically solved. List all the driving and restraining forces, as well as resources needed to increase the drive toward change.

Force Field Analysis

Problem Definition	Specific Goals
Driving Forces	Restraining Forces

Force Field Analysis *(Cont.)*

Driving Forces	Restraining Forces

Resources needed to strengthen the driving forces or to weaken the restraining forces.

Use this form to analyze the force field analysis from the previous page.

Second Rank Order of Importance	Goal		*Third* Rate: Clarity		
	First List all "for" and "against" forces below		Clear	Partly Clear	Unclear
Fourth Look at combination of ranking and rating					

Time Lines

Take the information from the force field analysis to plan a time line for action. You need to know what strategies and activities will move you toward your goal. On the following page is a sample design of a timeline used in planning a nonviolent demonstration at Burr Industries. Based upon this model, make one to use for getting a corporation or government body to alter its policies. Brainstorm specific strategies and activities, placing them on a time line with specific dates for activities to be accomplished. Also, add the initials of individuals from your group who will carry out specific responsibilities.

It is useful to place time lines on large sheets of newsprint, to make them highly visible as a constant reminder of dates and names of people responsible for accomplishing specific tasks. They are visible forms of accountability to help an organization move forward towards its collective goals. Be ready to share your timeline with others.

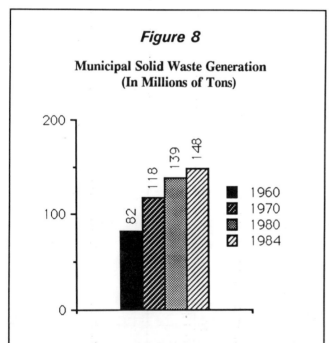

Figure 8

Municipal Solid Waste Generation
(In Millions of Tons)

1960 82
1970 118
1980 139
1984 148

Covers post-consumer residential and commercial solid wastes which comprise the major portion of typical municipal collections. Excludes mining, agricultural, and industrial processing, demolition and construction wastes, sewage sludge, and junked autos and obsolete equipment wastes. Based on material-flows estimating procedure and wet weight as generated.

U. S. Department of Commerce, Bureau of the Census, *Statistical Abstracts of the United States 1987,* 107th Edition. Washington D. C.: U.S. Government Printing Office, 1987.

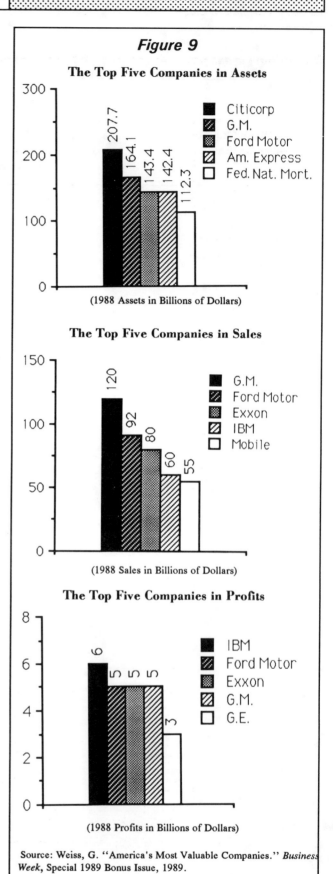

Figure 9

The Top Five Companies in Assets

Citicorp 207.7
G.M. 164.1
Ford Motor 143.4
Am. Express 142.4
Fed. Nat. Mort. 112.3

(1988 Assets in Billions of Dollars)

The Top Five Companies in Sales

G.M. 120
Ford Motor 92
Exxon 80
IBM 60
Mobile 55

(1988 Sales in Billions of Dollars)

The Top Five Companies in Profits

IBM 6
Ford Motor 5
Exxon 5
G.M. 5
G.E. 3

(1988 Profits in Billions of Dollars)

Source: Weiss, G. "America's Most Valuable Companies." *Business Week,* Special 1989 Bonus Issue, 1989.

Action*: Burr Industry

Activity/Event/Procedure	September	October	November	December	January
ORGANIZATIONAL MEETING	Sep. 25				
RADIO ANNOUNCEMENT OF MASS MEETING	Sep. 28 - Oct. 6				
FLYERS FOR MASS MEETING		Oct. 6 - 15			
MASS MEETING		Oct. 16			
RADIO ANNOUNCEMENT ON ACTION			Oct. 28 - Jan. 7		
FLYERS ON ACTION				Dec. 8 - Jan. 7	
PRESS CONFERENCE ON ACTION					Jan. 1
WORKSHOP ON NONVIOLENCE				Dec. 8	Jan. 1
NOTIFICATION OF POLICE AND LAWYERS OF ACTION					Jan. 1
ACTION					Jan. 5
EVALUATION					Jan. 7

* Action = Nonviolent Demonstration

Session Number Seven: Force Field Analysis

Objectives of the Session
To share corporate findings in mixed teams.

To provide opportunities for participants to present a force field analysis and a timeline for critique.

Design Flow in Minutes
5 minutes Agenda review.
60 minutes Participants to share information on their corporate research.
10 minutes Break.
35 minutes One or more teams to present their force field analysis and timeline for critique.
10 minutes Evaluation.

Homework
Thus far, our view of corporations comes from action research and other related experiences. We now turn to a view and analysis of corporate power to help put some of our action reseach in perspective. You may disagree with this analysis or perspective, but it is one that is worth putting forth for debate. This is not to say that all corporations fit into the perspective that is being advanced in concept paper III on *Corporate Power*; however, many of them do. Read *Corporate Power* and also concept paper IV, *A Conceptual Analylsis of Power for Social and Environmental Change,* and be prepared to discuss them at the next session. Also read the segment on *Risk Assessment and Nuclear Waste* and complete the *Risk Assessment Chart.*

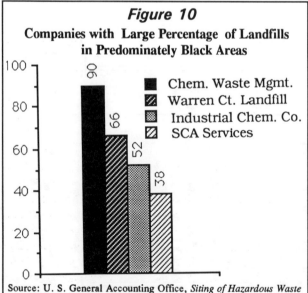

Figure 10
Companies with Large Percentage of Landfills in Predominately Black Areas

- Chem. Waste Mgmt.
- Warren Ct. Landfill
- Industrial Chem. Co.
- SCA Services

Source: U. S. General Accounting Office, *Siting of Hazardous Waste Landfills and their Correlation with Racial and Economic Status of Surrounding Communities.*. Washington D. C.: June 1, 1983, GAO/ RCED-83-168.

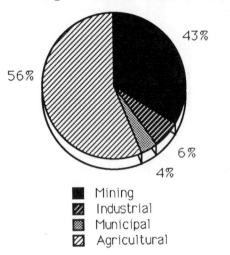

Figure 11
Sources of Solid Waste in U. S. in 1978 as a Percentage of the Total Wet Waste Produced

43%
56%
6%
4%

- Mining
- Industrial
- Municipal
- Agricultural

Source: Miller, G. T., Jr., *Living in the Environment,* Third Edition. Belmont, California: Wadsworth Publishing Company, 1982.

Figure 12
Public Opposition in Selected Countries to Building Additional Nuclear Power Plants

Country	Percent Opposed Before Chernobyl	After Chernobyl
U.K.	65	83
W. Germany	46	83
Italy	--	79
U.S.	67	78
Yugoslavia	40	74
Canada	60	70
Finland	33	64
France	--	52

Wording and polling techniques varied, but data are broadly comparable. Pre-Chernobyl figures are from pools taken between 1982 and 1986.

Source: Flavin, C. *Worldwatch Paper 75: Reassessing Nuclear Power: The Fallout From Chernobyl.* Washington D.C.: Worldwatch Institue, 1987.

Concept Paper III: Corporate Power

The industrial revolution of the 19th century created competition for raw materials, many of which were found in underdeveloped countries. European companies were chartered to exploit the vast untapped wealth of countries all over the world. Such competition caused wars over territorial rights and control of resources. Within our own country, vast supplies of natural resources were made available to companies, often as public subsidies. The seemingly endless supply of coal, oil, timber, and minerals juxtaposed with a pool of cheap migrant labor stimulated the growth of thousands of business enterprises.

At the end of the Civil War, scholar-activists, citizen groups, and volunteer organizations were concerned about the wanton destruction of the natural resources. This concern led to the conservation movement, which was eventually institutionalized by government to make it easier for corporate barons to enhance their profits. The U.S. government rather cheaply managed the land for industry's future use and profits. It was during the post-Civil War era that the railroads and expanded operations of the Rockefeller oil and Carnegie steel empires developed into modern industrial corporations. It was also during this period that the corporate system became increasingly concentrated, with entire industries dominated by a few large corporate entities (Corporate Guide, 1974).

The sources of corporate control are numerous; some have already been mentioned. Conglomerate corporations continued to grow in spite of one hundred years of government regulation, anti-trust actions, labor confrontations, and public concern. Corporate power in America was able to perpetuate a myth of fair competition and free enterprise by spending billions of dollars a year on public relations to gain public support.

Large corporations were rather successful in mergers that swallowed up their competition, consolidating their control over markets. Interlocking boards of directors--a method of having an executive sit on the board of directors of several corporations simultaneously--led to joint planning of corporations supposedly in competition with one another. Joint ventures, the creation of a company by two or more firms for particular business projects, is another mechanism used to pool capital to share risks and profits. These practices have most often led to the lessening of competition and to economic manipulation. Price fixing is nothing new on the American corporate scene; prices are fixed administratively rather than by the market.

The government was instrumental in helping corporations become powerful entities, though this has not always been the intent of government incumbents. The government spends billions of dollars each year to provide corporations with lucrative profits, many of which come in the form of cost overruns. Let's explore this further. The rate of profit on military work is much higher than on domestic work. In 1979, for example, Chrysler's profit rate on military work was 78 percent, while their civilian profit rate was a negative figure. Additionally, the average cost overrun of military contracts with private industry was 300 percent (Cyper, 1981), ensuring high rates of return. This may be considered a form of welfare for the rich, a way of enhancing their profits considerably with little, if any, risk.

Consolidation of Power

The government was helpful in the consolidation of corporate power in other ways, too. Although agencies such as the Interstate Commerce Commission, the Federal Power Commission, the Federal Communication Commission, the Securities and Exchange Commission, and the Civil Aeronautics Board were designed to regulate industry, they became dominated by corporate executives, the very people whom the agencies intended to monitor. The revolving door between these government agencies and corporations--that is, agency people retiring to corporate boardrooms and executive positions, and vice versa--places them in a position to manipulate commissions for their own particular economic interests.

The commissions often rely solely on corporations to give them information to determine violation of laws. In other instances, it takes years for a decision; commissions are usually understaffed or lack expertise. Even though attempts were made to regulate industry, rules and regulations served to protect large corporations. Such rules and regulations provided them with control over markets and resources they were never able to obtain by themselves. The net effect is that smaller industries are kept out of the market, because such rules and regulations require time and money for compliance.

Multi-national corporations pose economic and political problems for governments and people around the world. Often these corporations are so powerful they no longer have any allegiance to any one country. They are able to drastically influence the political economy of nations the world over. They exploit abundant resources and cheap labor in undeveloped countries (UDCs) for profit maximization. Conditions of workers are inferior to those in developed countries; often they are not allowed to strike for higher wages or safer work conditions.

The absence of environmental regulations in many

UDCs is an open invitation for the despoliation of their highly cherished natural resources. The dissemination of high technology, including the whole alphabet soup of chemicals, some of which are banned in our own country, affects the health of indigenous populations throughout the world. The sale of complex machines for agriculture and war keeps UDCs in a state of what political economists call structural dependency. Countries wishing to increase their gross national product find it rather difficult because of unfair trade advantages held by others. Frequently, U.S. loans to UDCs are used to purchase U.S. equipment and technology, a governmental subsidy to American corporations. The regressive tax structure found in UDCs means that the poor have to pay a disproportionate amount to offset the cost of loans.

The mechanization of farming causes considerable unemployment and suffering in UDCs. Thousands of people, once anchored to the land, now find themselves in overcrowded cities looking for work; thousands find themselves in abject poverty and victims of all the crimes that come from the plight of over-populated urban areas. People are starving. Fertile land that could grow food to feed indigenous populations is used to grow cash crops for distant ports. Most of the land is owned by elite groups or by multinational corporations. Over the years, multinationals gained control of large tracts of land to serve their economic interests. Thus, many of the liberation movements taking place in these countries have to do with human dignity and land tenure questions. A redistribution of land on a more equitable basis can provide people with the means for food and shelter. Land tenure is at the core of the dissatisfaction among the poor and the disenfranchised.

Growth and Development

Multinational corporations not only had an impact on UDCs, but also on Europe through the Marshall Plan. The Marshall Plan not only helped war-torn Europe to recover economically, but it also provided new market penetration for American corporations. Charles Wilson, head of the War Production Board, recommended that we embark upon a "permanent wartime economy to make sure that our defense systems are ever ready" to protect our corporations so they could expand and prosper (Corporate Guide, 1974). This was the beginning of the military-industrial complex and the Cold War, which have had a profound effect upon this country and the world as a whole. The burgeoning defense industry was basically supported by American citizens to stave off the threat of communism. This was a perfect fit, i.e., a strong military to protect the free world and profits.

The climate was right for growth and development. Oil companies were recipients of tax allowances and cred-

its. They eventually took over fertilizer, coal, nuclear power, chemicals, and plastic industries. Following the 1950s, conglomerates dominated the corporate scene, seeking and gaining control over a wide range of often diverse products. Two hundred corporations dominated over fifty percent of markets, assets, and profits in the 1970s. For instance, General Motors profits exceeded the gross national products of all but twenty-one of the largest countries of the world. With this unprecedented growth and development has come unprecedented political power that is used to gain multiple concessions from countries the world over.

But these corporations need support of citizens to maintain their power and world hegemony. U.S. taxpayers are the largest underwriters of industrial research and development. Billions of dollars are spent annually on research and development within our nation. Private industries receive the lion's share of research and development monies from the Department of Defense and the National Aeronautics and Space Administration. Governmental subsidies in this form increase both profit and power of conglomerates, undermining our own sense of freedom and democracy. It is such subsidies that provide opportunities without risk for corporations to explore new horizons at the taxpayer's expense. If such enterprises fail, then they are written off as a taxpayer's loss; if they are successful, then corporations make millions in spin-off projects. With this kind of support and a strong military, it is almost impossible for large corporate power to fail in the U.S. or on foreign soil. So, in a sense, corporations are public institutions, dependent upon public monies for research to increase their profit margins. They depend on the public for labor to produce goods and services and upon the public to buy them. Yet decisions affecting millions of people are often made in secrecy in corporate boardrooms (Corporate Guide, 1974). More and more people are beginning to question the nature and the role of corporations and their sense of social responsibility.

Organized Labor

Organized labor is the major countervailing force against corporate power in the United States. The growth of organized labor is a bloody page in the history of the nineteenth and twentieth centuries. Corporate power used bullets, strike-breakers, and bribes to thwart the organizing of workers to improve their working conditions and wages. However, ultimately, this was to no avail. Unions grew in strength. During President Franklin Roosevelt's New Deal, collective bargaining became a legitimate and powerful tool of unions to win concessions from management. Yet now, we see the once powerful unions eroding in the face of changing times. The internationalization of capital, whereby corporations invest in UDCs for cheaper labor and abundant resources, leaves American workers preoccupied with plant closings and plant relocation. High technology is replacing workers at alarming rates. Although it creates new jobs for some, there will be a net loss of jobs, creating welfare-dependent workers. Unions have fewer workers to pay union dues and fewer workers to stop production and, thus, fewer workers to back them in collective bargaining.

Labor is not the only organized attempt to resist corporate decision-making. Environmentalists, too, have resisted production policies of corporate power. Often, the by-products of production--management mistakes, accidents, preoccupation with enhancing corporate profits, or war--may cause a considerable amount of damage to both the environment and health. By 1980, more than 1,200 Vietnam veterans filed claims with the U.S. Veterans Administration for disabilities based on their exposure to Agent Orange, a defoliant used in the war to clear the jungles. They had medical symptoms such as liver damage, muscular weakness, testicular cancer, numbness, loss of sex drive, skin disease, sleep and mood disturbances, and birth defects in offspring. Such herbicides as 2, 4, 5-T and Silvex, a related chemical, were banned in the United States in 1979 as a result of abnormally high incidence of miscarriages in women. Air pollution is hard on people, particularly the young, the poor, and people living in close proximity to its source. Multiple diseases, such as bronchitis, emphysema, lung cancer, stomach cancer, or heart disease, are caused or made worse by such pollutants. Nitrous oxides released from nitrogen fertilizer can eliminate the ozone layer, thus causing increased skin cancer. Our ground water, rivers, lakes, and oceans are threatened by industrial pollutants. Half of U.S. citizens depend upon their ground water for drinking, while others depend upon rivers and lakes (Miller, 1982). Environmentalists find just cause in undertaking multiple resistance to corporate decisions that threaten to do harm to life here on earth.

We Can Do Better

Corporations will always be with us, at least in the foreseeable future. They are instrumental in providing goods and services to people. We think they can do better. Goods and services can be produced in a manner that is more protective of the environment and human dignity. We can no longer make colossal mistakes as we did at Love Canal, with PBBs in Michigan, with toxic dump sites that pollute our underground water tables, or with nuclear power plants and the handling of their by-products. We can no longer make these mistakes because it might cause human and environmental tragedies beyond our wildest comprehension--tragedies that will be with us for centuries to come. There is no conspiracy on the part of corporations to do the species harm, but, in a society

that is propelled by economic growth and profit, science and technology, production and efficiency, a considerable amount of damage may be done to our planet earth. Also, concentrations of corporate power in this country often make corporations oblivious to the impact of their decision-making upon the social order. Corporate decisions cause thousands to suffer from pollution in communities and in the workplace; they cause thousands to be unemployed and relocated in distant communities; they cause hundreds of communities to decay by their withdrawal of taxes and corporate relocation to other parts of the U.S. or the Third World.

This critique of corporate power in America is rather harsh; it has to be in a world that is determined by high technology and economic growth, in a world that brings into existence chemicals and synthetics that could threaten our very survival here on earth. We can do better, and we must. If we do not, we will surely perish as millions of species have done throughout history.

Everyone cannot be expected to work outside traditional institutions. Most of us will probably work within them. They will be a large part of our lives and the lives of our loved ones and friends. Often, there will be instances where organizational activities may be in conflict with personal values. This is not to indicate that all organizations are engaged in some illegal or unethical activity. Sometimes they are, but most times not. Most organizations try to adhere to ethical norms and standards. In some instances, things run afoul, leaving one in conflict with organizational activities. Sometimes going through organizational channels does not provide bold relief. Both professional and lay people are sometimes motivated to take action by going outside their organizations to get them to respond appropriately. Some people pay a high price for blowing the whistle on their bosses. They not only lose their jobs and homes, but their careers are destroyed, leaving their families to suffer.

Whistle-Blowing

Whistle-blowing, however, is becoming more acceptable. An alarmed public is more sensitive to secret corporate contributions that corrupt the American government and the political process. Changes in social values and lifestyle encourage whistle-blowing. A new sense of activism, as well as personal and moral commitment, grew out of civil rights, anti-war, consumer, and social protest movements. There is an increased concern that professional employees should not be forced to perform services that would clearly violate their ethical standards. There is growing awareness that corporate behavior can have serious effects upon the public and our highly cherished environment. The enactment of a dozen major employee protection and public policy laws by Congress and the states adds incentive for employees to act upon their own values, even though they may be contrary to corporate ones. These laws encourage whistle-blowing.

Don Gillert, a pilot for 25 years, with over one-third of those years with Eastern Airlines, blew the whistle on serious defects in the Lockheed L-1011 wide-body aircraft. Eastern Airlines management failed to respond to Gillert's warning and, a few months later, the problem played a key role in the crash of an Eastern L-1011 in which 103 people were killed. Joseph Rose, a young attorney well on his way to corporate success, exposed overpayments to lawyers by the Association of Milk Producers (AMPI). The attorneys, in turn, kicked back money to AMPI officials for political use. This became known as the "Milk Deal," in which AMPI, along with other smaller dairy cooperatives, made a series of illegal corporate contributions to Richard Nixon's 1972 reelection campaign in exchange for a raise in federal milk price supports. Rose lost his job, and came fairly close to losing his career as a lawyer.

Peter Faulkner, working for the Nuclear Services Corporation as a system-application engineer, wrote a paper for the U.S. Senate Subcommittee on Engineering Deficiencies in nuclear power systems that were currently being used or on the market. Three weeks later he was fired. These are only a few examples of whistle-blowing. Hundreds more are doing it or anticipate doing it (Westin, 1981).

Questions

In what way is the analysis of corporate power in this article similar or dissimilar to your responses to and discussion of the questionnaire which you completed at the beginning of this manual?

In what way is the article similar or dissimilar to your own analysis of your research data on corporations?

Given the power of these corporations, such as interlocking boards of directors, unfair competitive activities, and weak regulatory commissions, what is your analysis of them from a power-conflict perspective?

What would be your solutions for controlling corporate power that operates outside the law or engages in questionable activities?

What a Trillion and a Half Dollars for the Pentagon Will Mean for You

The $1.6 billion it cost to build one Trident Nuclear Submarine...Could restore the $1.3 billion cut from fiscal year 1982 Mass Transit subsidies.

The $40 billion for the 100 B-1 bombers requested by Reagan...Would pay the cost of a comprehensive ten-year energy-efficiency effort to cut oil imports by 20 to 35 percent.

The $2.1 billion it costs to build one CVN-71 Nuclear Carrier...Could restore full funding for Medicaid (cut by $900 million), and Aid to Families with Dependent Children (cut by $1.2 billion).

The $8.4 billion in cost escalations in 1981 on the AEGIS Cruiser program...Would fund the comprehensive research and development needed to produce 80- to 100-mile-per-gallon cars.

The $400 million authorized for development of the Pershing II missile system...Could restore the $352 million cut from health education and training programs.

Funds totaling one-thirteenth of fiscal year 1982 military spending increase over 1981 levels ($5 billion)... Could restore full funding for Food Stamps (cut by $1.7 billion), Child Nutrition (cut by $1.5 billion), and unemployent benefits (cut by $1.7 billion).

The extra $13 billion spent on the XM-1 Tank program through 1981 due to cost escalations...Would provide the funds needed to rehabilitate New York City's transit system ($6.8 billion) and sewer system ($5.1 billion).

The $121 million it costs to build two KC-10A Cargo Planes...Could save the National Endowment for the Arts and the National Endowment for the Humanities from a combined cut of $113 million.

(Source: Coalition for a New Foreign and Military Policy. Undated.)

Concept Paper IV:
A Conceptual Analysis of Power for Social and Environment Change

Thus far we have articulated the differences between conflict I and conflict II, highlighting their strengths and limitations. We have also made an analysis of corporate power and the role it plays in society. In this section, social and political power are addressed to help us understand some of their forms. Power may be a means for solving conflict by one party forcing its will upon another or a means by which parties with equal amounts of power are forced to negotiate with one another.

Social power is the capacity to control the behavior of others and institutions--sometimes directly and sometimes indirectly. It refers to influence, pressure, and coercion by power holders to implement or to achieve certain desired ends. Even nonviolent action can be a form of power which seeks to reduce the power of antagonists, as evidenced by the variety of nonviolent demonstrations that have been successfully used in this country.

The labor movement has historically participated in strikes and work stoppages to enhance their collective bargaining ability, getting management to improve upon working conditions and wages. The civil rights movement consciously and nonviolently broke unjust laws, which had kept minorities in a state of oppression, and raised the consciousness of millions of people to take action against such laws regarding education, housing, and employment. The anti-nuclear movement was successful in drawing attention to the builders of nuclear power plants by slowing down their construction or stopping their development.

Some Assumptions

At this point, it is important that assumptions about power be articulated to help with strategies for social and environmental change (SEC). To increase understandings of power, we articulate two underlying assumptions. The first is that power comes from the top, from those at the apex of society or from those with wealth and political connections. It assumes that people are dependent upon powerful elite groups or governments or some hierarchical system to provide structure and order in their lives. Often we view government and national and multi-national corporations with their billion-dollar assets as being beyond our reach to change or influence. They have considerable power that extends throughout the world. Such power seems to be durable, self-perpetuating, not easily controlled or destroyed. Thus, our assumptions about power become the framework by which we analyze society for intentional social change. For instance, if we assume power is emitted from the top and is durable and self-perpetuating, then armed struggle or violence may result in

changing power relations in society (Sharpe, 1973).

The other assumption made about power is that hierarchical systems are dependent upon people supporting them. Such hierarchical systems could not exist without popular support or a willingness to cooperate with the people in power. Therefore, power is viewed as fragile and not durable. Its strength is dependent upon the cooperation of the masses. If we assume that power comes from the consent of the people, then the withdrawal of that consent becomes a rather powerful means for people to act collectively to alter power relations in society (Sharpe, 1973). Historically, civil disobedience, boycotts, and other forms of demonstrations and non-cooperation have been used by multiple groups, and rather successfully. If we assume that political power is dependent upon the cooperation of people, then this undoubtedly sets the framework for nonviolent direct-action strategies for intentional social change.

Empowerment

Most people are law-abiding for numerous reasons: 1) Well-established law becomes the norm for people to abide by even if it's a "bad" one; 2) fear of sanctions is used to thwart actions that may run contrary to law; 3) obedience to government is perceived as being for the common good to prevent social chaos; 4) emotional identification with leaders is a powerful force that influences the positive behavior of millions of people; and 5) self-interests are motivating factors in that people cooperate with those in power for status, prestige, position, or rewards (Sharpe, 1973).

The absence of confidence to change power relations is prevalent among the disenfranchised. In most instances, those in power, such as bureaucrats and middle managers, use obedience and cooperation to help control and influence the populace. These are only some of the reasons why people obey; this list is by no means inclusive.

Sharpe (1973) assumes that the degree of power invested in elite groups is dependent upon the relative desire of the populace to be controlled. A well-informed and active group can make meaningful demands upon antagonists by withholding their consent to prevent them from governing. At times the populace reacts with apathy; other times, they become political in character. A small number of people experienced empowerment by withdrawing their consent to the war in Vietnam, or by resisting racially segregated schools, or by protesting the arms race and nuclear power plant construction. People are building independent voluntary organizations to empower themselves to resist or change certain government and corporate policies. Before going further, let's analyze the bases of power.

Bases of Power

The base of power is not power itself. It is only power if perceived by people as being important to them, i.e., being important enough to influence their behavior. For example, if money is not important to individuals, then it's rather difficult for money to be used to influence behavior. Money is only a base of power, not power itself. French and Raven address five bases of power--legitimate, reward, coercive, referent, and expert--to help us understand the bases of power and how they are used to exert power. These bases of power will be explored in this section.

Legitimate. This base of power is often the most difficult to explain. It is usually associated with authority in which people, through their position, have rights to make certain decisions. It is the right to command or be obeyed by others; it is the voluntary acceptance of an action by a person in authority. A person having legitimate power may not necessarily be more competent than one without it. Also, a Congressperson representing our voting preferences has legitimacy to act in our self-interests. Lobbyists from Environmental Action or Friends of the Earth or the Wilderness Society have legitimacy to represent their membership on Capitol Hill. A person we elect as president of some organization has legitimate power. Legitimacy is derived from a number of different sources. It comes from high-level people within organizations that delegate authority, it comes from a body of law, or it comes from degrees conferred upon us. The recipients of influence perceive decisions and commands from a person as legitimate.

Reward. The ability to control rewards is also a base for power. These bases of influence are cultivated by our culture. Culture often determines what is rewarding for us to do, buy, or cherish. Control over property is a way of assessing wealth, privilege, and power. Money, stocks, bonds, and portfolio investments often indicate the potential influence of people. Control of natural resources, namely, minerals and forest products, is the basis for wealth and power. Political connections and political patronage serve as bases to influence people to gain party loyalty. In a highly affluent society like ours, there are many material bases for reward power. People and corporations which control great rewards have considerable influence over our daily lives, our foreign and domestic policies, and our government. In 1983, the richest one percent of adults or families held 34.3 percent of the wealth. If people decided to embrace a nonmaterial society, and if they re-evaluated what is important to them, this would perhaps weaken the power grip of the few over the masses. But this would take a considerable amount of consciousness-raising and unrelenting commitment.

Coercive. Coercion is another base of power that is widely used in society. It is the ability to use certain sanctions to control and direct behavior. Economic boycotts and embargoes are frequently used by governments for certain prescribed ends. Bombings and military invasions are coercive measures used to punish people and nation-states that break with traditional political conformity. In other instances, dissident groups use terrorism to force political settlements or to make known injustices of various political regimes. On the domestic scene, strikes, political noncooperation, boycotts, demonstrations, and civil disobedience are effectively used to gain political and economic concessions. Violence, in particular, is a form of coercion used in our society to punish or to force people to respond in a given direction. The state uses a considerable amount of coercion to maintain law and order. Sometimes the maintenance of law and order does not mean that justice is served. Coercion was historically used in this country to keep minorities in their place. People are often willing to undergo coercion or sanction to change those conditions responsible for their oppression. Coercion is fairly common to the American landscape.

Referent. This power comes from the identification of the masses with some popular leader. Such leaders are able to exert influence because people find them attractive. Such attractiveness may be related to physical attributes, personal charisma, or ideology. In other instances, we are attracted to people because of their prestige or knowledge. For example, President John F. Kennedy captured the hearts and minds of millions, mostly through his personal appeal. Mao was able to attract and influence millions of people in China because of his revolutionary ideology. These two leaders were polar opposites in their world outlook but, nonetheless, commanded a considerable amount of influence and power. Martin Luther King and Jesse Jackson are or have been referents: through their power they were able to influence millions of people to support the cause of justice and political equality in this country. This identification may be stronger when common beliefs or sense of purpose have broken down or when people need someone or something to believe in, something to give them hope and guidance. President Ronald Reagan may have fulfilled this need for millions of Americans.

Expert. Elite groups are dependent upon middle managers and people with specialized knowledge and skills. Without such skills, many elite and powerful groups could not survive; they are dependent upon the expertise of scientists, university professors, researchers, technocrats, and others to make their investments safe or to increase capital accumulation. (Few, if any, Nobel Prizes come from the upper crust of society; most of them come from middle and upper middle classes, at best.) Elite groups hire and pay well for the expertise they need. For instance, if welfare mothers had the money of elite groups, they, too, could hire expertise to make a significant contribution to society. In addition, expert power is highly revered in our society. It is supported by our culture. Research and technology made us number one in the world. Therefore, the withdrawal of expert power can become a significant force for SEC.

Popular Noncooperation

Noncooperation by the masses under certain conditions creates serious political problems for government and elite groups. It is rather difficult for people to be oppressed by tyrannical governments unless they become accomplices and, at the same time, victims. Government or elite groups cannot survive without consent of the masses. The upper class could not engage in capital accumulation or conspicuous consumption unless people beneath them provided the necessary labor and services. The task of organizers is to help people free themselves through consciousness-raising dialogue. Knowledge of their power has to be used to free themselves as well as the oppressor.

Getting people to participate in civil disobedience or noncooperation is no easy matter. People are usually wedded to a system of oppression out of habit, out of moral obligation, out of fear of reprisals from those in power, or out of their own sense that they have neither the skill nor desire to alter their relationship with those responsible for their condition. It takes considerable time and skill to get people to act in their own behalf (Sharpe, 1973).

Not only does power corrupt, but powerlessness corrupts, too. Feelings of insignificance and apathy are often found among those without power. Alienation and despair come from a sense of helplessness in controlling their lives. People feel incapable of engaging in multiple resistance or in activities to empower themselves.

Often violence is the ultimate state of powerlessness; it becomes the last resort for self-esteem and significance, putting us in touch with our metaphysical being. But people can empower themselves without resorting to violence. Violence often begets more violence. Empowerment can be developed through a number of noncooperation and nonviolent direct-action means. It is rather difficult to organize people if too much powerlessness has eaten away at the core of their self-esteem and their sense of who they are. It can be done.

Power and Acceptance

Gamson (1975) spends time attempting to measure outcomes of acceptance of the challenging group by antagonists. He is interested in whether the relationship between the challenging group and its antagonists change during the course of the challenge. Although more complicated, according to Gamson, acceptance involves a change from hostility or indifference to a more positive relationship between antagonists and challengers. He thus describes four kinds of relationships: 1) consultation, 2) negotiation, 3) formal recognition, and 4) inclusion.

Although Gamson reports on four indicators of positive relations between what he calls the challenging group and the antagonist, this relationship is deeply rooted in the bases of power. Without the bases of power, such relationships could not exist in any meaningful way. What are the bases of power that underlie the acceptance of challengers by antagonists? An antagonist *legitimizes* the challenging group by asking them to participate as a consultant *(expert)* in some form or fashion. In other instances, the relationship can be characterized by the antagonist expressing explicitly, typically in writing, that it *recognizes* the challenging group as being *legitimate* representatives of a given constituency. If an antagonist *recognizes* a group as the *legitimate negotiating* agent for a certain constituency, it probably does so because of the power of the challenging group to cooperate with antagonists *(reward)* or the power of the challenging group to withhold cooperation *from antagonists (coercive)*. And the antagonist may include the challenging group because it has several bases of power, such as expert, reward, coercive, (it may be better to include them and solicit their cooperation than not include them), legitimate and referent (personal power that comes from influence that is independent of an organization or constituency position).

While the antagonist may include the challenging group within its organizational structure, it is essential that it maintain its own status and identity. If serving in the antagonist's organization requires repudiating membership in the challenging group as a condition of office, it is more like co-optation rather than a relationship through inclusion.

When the antagonists legitimize the challengers as consultants, they are also perceiving them as experts--experts with specialized knowledge to make a significant contribution. When the antagonist is willing to enter into negotiations with the challenging group, i.e., on a continuous basis and not just during crisis conditions, the relationship implies that the challenging group is the legitimate representative of a given constituency. The underlying power base is one of both coercion and reward. In order for antagonists to enter into such a relationship, they must perceive the challenging group to have both coercive and reward power--that is, the power to disrupt the on-going routines of the antagonist's organization or to make life difficult for them in some way. Or they perceive challenging groups as potential for rewards through cooperation, peace, and normalized relations. The same arguments can be made for inclusison of the challenging group or its leaders.

Questions

In what ways do you agree or disagree with the assumptions made about power in this article? What is your own assumption about power?

Give specific examples of the power bases that underly acceptance of challengers by antagonists?

In what ways can nonviolence and noncooperation be used to change powerful corporate policies in this country? Can nonviolence be used to bring about broad-based fundamental change in this country? What about throughout the world?

Do you believe in nonviolence as a philosophy or as a strategy? Explain.

Many of the ideas in this paper come from: Sharpe, G. *The Politics of Nonviolent Action.* Boston: Porter Sargent, 1973.

The "bases of power" information comes from: French, J. R. P., and Raven, B., "The Bases of Power," in Cartwright, D., and Zander, A., *Group Dynamics: Research and Theory.* New York: Harper and Row, 1960, third edition.

Risk Assessment and Nuclear Waste

What would you do to end these dangerous pollutants in your community? Following is a list of possible actions you could take. Place a plus (+) by those you would be willing to risk. Place a minus (-) by statements you feel are too risky for you. Place a (0) by statements you are unsure about. Share your answers when finished in small groups.

( ) Write a letter to your congressperson.

( ) Write letters to editors of local newspapers.

( ) Work for the election of an environmentalist to public office.

( ) Take on a more active role in an environmental group, such as leader of a task force to eliminate toxic substances in the environment.

( ) Participate in a vigil or demonstration.

( ) Spend time distributing leaflets downtown or at a shopping center.

( ) Circulate a petition downtown or door-to-door.

( ) Organize a campaign to get a local company to stop polluting or find safe methods of handling its waste.

( ) Visit corporate management and boards of directors to confront them on their policies.

( ) Encourage people to boycott the products of the company until it changes its policy.

( ) Perform a citizen's arrest of a corporate executive.

( ) Quit your job for a year and work to change company policies.

( ) Disrupt a stockholders meeting.

( ) Participate in the destruction of company property.

( ) Respond to violence with violence.

( ) Join a mass nonviolent civil disobedience action to get companies to change their policies.

On the next page, fill out the *Risk and Commitment Chart* individually and then discuss it in small groups. Discuss what these risks mean to you personally. Remember, not everyone is prepared to take the same risks. It is easy to fantasize risks, yet become paralyzed by their reality. Participants should push each other to take some risks. You should also ask each other what support groups would allow you to take certain risks. Now, think about risks you are willing to take, and check the appropriate sections of the chart.

Risk and Commitment Chart

Kinds of risks	What I am committed to risk to stop toxic dump sites	Probability of this risk eventually occurring
1) Economic loss		
2) Physical danger		
3) Loss of self-esteem		
4) Legal action		
5) Loss of political credibility		
6) Professional sanctions		
7) Career threats		
8) _____		
9) _____		
10) _____		

Session Number Eight: Power and Risk

Objectives of the Session
To provide opportunities to discuss the concept papers on *Corporate Power* and *A Conceptual Analysis of Power for Social and Environmental Change.*

To improve your conceptual and operational understanding of power and nonviolence.

To discuss your risk assessment responses.

Design Flow in Minutes
5 minutes   Agenda review.
45 minutes   Answer and discuss questions at the end of the two concept papers. This is to be done in small groups.
35 minutes   Discussion (small groups/mixed teams) of the *Risk and Commitment Chart.*
5 minutes   Evaluation.
5 minutes   Form groups of three each.
35 minutes   Share your individual responses to the *Risk and Commitment Chart.*

Homework
The media have become increasingly important in social and environmental change. Their power definitely affects us all. Corporations, politicians, and governments have all learned to use the power of media rather effectively. Also nonprofit organizations or community groups are becoming more skilled in using the media for certain desired outcomes.

The use of media becomes important for building organizations for advocacy planning. Such activities give visibility to organizations and the issues they support, drawing people into the organization who might never have been attracted otherwise. To consider such activities, read the concept paper on *Media and Social and Environmental Change* and the information on public service announcements, as well as the sample news release and press conference items. Plan a media strategy by using the skills and strategies on these following pages.

Concept Paper V: Media and Social and Environmental Change

Conflict or exercising power cannot take place unless there is communication. Mass media becomes the major vehicle for augmenting conflict or power by its ability to transmit messages to large numbers of people almost instantaneously. Communication is a powerful tool that plays a major role in social and environmental change (SEC). Whether operating from conflict theories I or II or engaged in nonviolent noncooperation, civil disobedience, or war, communication becomes key for realizing success. The national media engages millions of people, increasing their awareness of societal issues. Media coverage may be used to widen the arena of conflict for additional support for SEC. The use of dogs, water hoses, and police against black women and children in Selma, Alabama, during a nonviolent demonstration in the 1960s was disseminated on TV. And enraged millions of Americans, many of whom went to Selma to lend support to the civil rights movement. Viewing the Vietnam War by telecommunications helped change millions of peoples' attitudes about that war. The publicity about the dangers of nuclear power plants increased resistance to building such structures. And certainly, thousands of people demonstrating against the arms race undoubtedly have had an effect upon attitudes of a much larger aggregate of people.

In times of war, the media plays an important role. For example, the war in Lebanon between Israel and the Palestinians was a media war, with each side attempting to gain support of the world community by interpreting and sharing in the media its own perception of the war. The Falkland Island crisis was another example out of which came two sets of contradictory data, with both sides trying to convince the public they were winning. The media can undoubtedly play a significant role in current events, even the winning of wars.

The world has become smaller. It's our technological extension of consciousness through electronic media and printed words that connects us with events almost as fast as they happen. Events happening in the world seem as though they are taking place in our neighborhoods; events happening in one city become the interest and concern of the world community; and people of different lands become our intimate neighbors. Media also help to keep government and politics both honest and accountable.

Media should be used to the fullest extent, because antagonists or political regimes engaging in questionable activities seldom want exposure. Media highlights their wrongdoings, thus making them respond to world opinion, scrutiny, and political pressures. Yet the absence of such coverage gives those in power a license to be more forthright in their brutal oppression of dissenters. The media not only increase the awareness and political support of resistors, but protect those involved in direct-action nonviolent campaigns. The price political regimes may pay for oppression is often weighed against world opinion. However, we must keep in mind that this does not always work.

Shaping Lifestyles

Media also play an important role in shaping buying habits, cultivating tastes, and shaping lifestyles. With corporations paying billions of dollars for advertisements to hustle their commodities to people (advertising that appeals to some of our most basic human drives, whetting our appetites for impulsive buying) we have become a society of conspicuous consumers, and a wasteful one at that. If we had less sex appeal in advertisements, we would be less motivated to buy things we do not want or seldom use. This is another example of the power of media to manipulate our buying habits.

But effective communication is more than just getting exposure or getting a large number of lines in print; it has to do with influencing attitudes and behaviors. Although communication ads and strategies might appeal to us personally, they may do just that and nothing else. An ad may be sophisticated, costing lots of money, but that does not mean it reaches the intended audience. Appealing to people to change their attitudes requires a great deal of planning, time, and energy.

Social science research helps us understand attitude change more fully. People with definite views on a subject will probably not change them, no matter how effective we think our campaign strategies are. People with firmly held views may use multiple defenses to protect themselves from influence, by rationalizing their behavior or attitudes, by failing to comprehend the argument from the opposing side, by ignoring it, or by forgetting it. People tend to seek information to fit into their value framework. They ignore conflicting information.

Corporations have become very astute in selling commodities, some of which we seldom need. They have used the power of social science and the media, creating needs where they didn't exist before to increase their sales and profits. Can environmentalists and organizers learn from corporate advertising strategies?

Communication Models

In the following section we explore four communication models that may prove to have some merit for environmental and grass-roots community organizations.

The Information Model. This model is fairly obvious. It is used to communicate directly with parties, taking the form of lectures, personal conversations, talk shows, group discussions, time on the 6:00 news, and simple ads. Most of the above may be used by organizers to inform people with the aim of building a grass-roots constituency. While many ads are expensive, they don't have to be; less "slick" ads are good to reinforce existing attitudes and behavior. They may not be good for changing attitudes, but they are rational attempts to both legitimize and reinforce existing behavior. While millions of people make a conscious effort to protect the environment, they periodically need to be convinced they are doing the right thing to remain active. Media ads can serve the purpose of mobilizing people to keep them active by legitimizing their work as important. Ads become important for networking, providing support to disconnected groups of people working for SEC. They let people know there are others out there who are just as concerned as they are (Sandman, 1976).

The Advertisers' Model. This model is used extensively by corporations to enhance their sales. Changing people's behavior is based upon reinforcing something within them that already exists. The questions to be asked are: What is that something that already exists within them? How can it be used to change their behavior? This is no easy matter to be sure. We start by listing basic drives common to all of us. Basic drives that appeal to needs are food, sex, thirst, sleep, and clean environments. While ads in newspapers, in magazines, and on television appeal to one or more basic drives, there is no rational relation between the behavior being urged and the need being appealed to. This behavior change model seldom depends upon logic. People buy cars, not because of cars per se, but because beautiful women in car ads suggest that owning cars like the one in the ads attracts beautiful women. The Madison and Fifth Avenue commercial advertisers appeal to our need states, getting us to spend billions we might not have spent otherwise (Sandman, 1976).

Cognitive Dissonance. Another way of creating behavioral change is by creating cognitive dissonance. This theory is based upon people's need to be consistent, or at least see themselves as consistent. Because people experience inconsistency (dissonance), they may feel tension; they become motivated to reduce such tensions. For example, people usually go through a series of rational steps comparing computers before purchasing one, checking with neighbors, computer magazines, TV ads, salespersons, etc. They eventually narrow the choice down to two or three computers, with no rational reason for purchasing

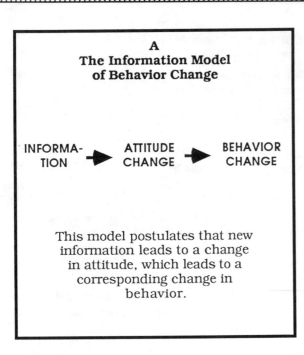

A
**The Information Model
of Behavior Change**

INFORMA-TION → ATTITUDE CHANGE → BEHAVIOR CHANGE

This model postulates that new information leads to a change in attitude, which leads to a corresponding change in behavior.

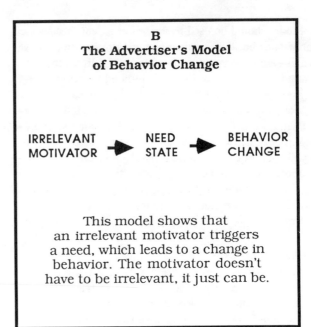

B
**The Advertiser's Model
of Behavior Change**

IRRELEVANT MOTIVATOR → NEED STATE → BEHAVIOR CHANGE

This model shows that an irrelevant motivator triggers a need, which leads to a change in behavior. The motivator doesn't have to be irrelevant, it just can be.

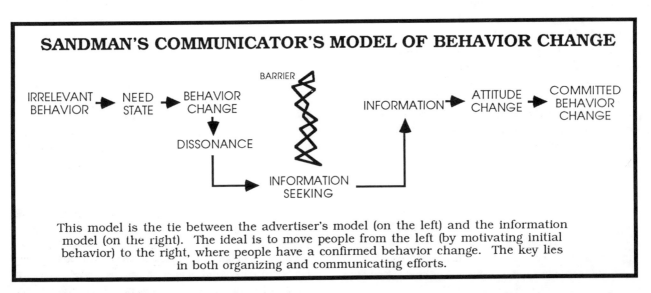

SANDMAN'S COMMUNICATOR'S MODEL OF BEHAVIOR CHANGE

IRRELEVANT BEHAVIOR → NEED STATE → BEHAVIOR CHANGE → DISSONANCE → INFORMATION SEEKING

BARRIER

INFORMATION → ATTITUDE CHANGE → COMMITTED BEHAVIOR CHANGE

This model is the tie between the advertiser's model (on the left) and the information model (on the right). The ideal is to move people from the left (by motivating initial behavior) to the right, where people have a confirmed behavior change. The key lies in both organizing and communicating efforts.

any one of the three. Because the decision may not be based upon rationality, they may not be entirely comfortable with buying, let's say, a Zenith. Once the behavioral commitment is made, they spend time seeking out positive information to justify their choice. Suddenly, they are not only more aware of Zeniths, but what people have to say about them. Making sense out of purchasing behavior becomes a minor preoccupation. Or take smoking, for instance. A well-developed and rational understanding of the harmful effects of smoking is common among millions of people. But their strong behavioral commitment to smoking makes their

inconsistency tolerable to them. Only if people come to be uncomfortable with their inconsistency is there motivation to change their attitudes, making them consistent with their behavior (Sandman, 1976).

Sandman's Model. Sandman (1976) combines the information model and the advertiser's model along with cognitive dissonance to create yet another model for behavior change. He suggests that appealing to a need that already exists can create a behavioral change, at which point the person experiences dissonance. If the behavior does not make sense, this is the time to provide rational information. People often seek information to make their behavior consistent with their attitudes or beliefs. The problem, however, with Sandman's model and the advertiser's model is they can become very expensive unless considerable amounts of creativity are used.

Application to SEC

Sandman states that the use of media does not replace organizing, but it can be a useful tool to help it along. The media get people to express an interest in doing something or asking for information. The media can not only generate supporters to join the organization, but can provide constant reinforcement for active members.

Sandman also uses an example of organizing by getting people to sign petitions (he treats this as a media event). He states that the most effective way is to ask people straight out to sign petitions, followed immediately by giving them information. Research shows that initial behavioral commitment (dissonance) followed up with information is a most effective way to get people involved in social change. He suggests that organizations are more likely to get long-term supporters if recruits signed knowing little, as opposed to knowing lots, about the issues. If they are not quite sure why they signed, they need more information, creating an opportunity to persuade them to become actively committed. Petitions also make good mailing lists, providing organizations have the means of getting back to remind people what they signed and the behavioral commitment they made. A thank-you card showing how they helped win a campaign and dates of future meetings may be helpful.

Appropriate Uses
of Behavioral Change Models

For change agents, the most important communication question to address is when to use the information, the advertiser's, or Sandman's model to influence people. In situations of immediate threat to one's self or body, it is too risky to depend upon the latter two models to provide the necessary safety. Rational information helps protect people engaged in nonviolent demonstrations by widening their base of support. For example, if media coverage had been absent during the most intense nonviolent conflicts in the 1960s, they would probably have ended in more, rather than less, violence. Antagonists are reluctant to use violence in the face of media; it holds them accountable to the broader public. Press conferences, letters to the editor, public hearings, and TV coverage using the information model are necessary to gain political pressures to protect activists engaged in direct-action nonviolent demonstrations. These messages are logical and clear, calling people's attention to issues under protest. These media activities garner support for those risking their lives at the center of direct-action campaigns. They encourage those in power to be reluctant to use brute force without dire consequence.

In those situations where there is no threatening orientation, a different approach may be more effective. Using the advertiser or Sandman's model may be more appropriate, particularly if used for ads, PSAs, slide shows, and the like. Using such models can be effective in getting people who are marginal to take that one giant step in the direction of SEC. The following materials on media techniques and methods emphasize the information model and/ or practical steps for gaining media access.

Question

How realistic is Sandman's communication model for challenging grass-roots groups involved in social change? What are its strengths and weaknesses?

Ideas in this concept paper have been taken primarily from: Sandman, P. *Mass Media,* a publication of the Northern Rockies Action Group, October 1976.

Public Service Announcements

Because public service announcements (PSAs) are a free way for social change groups to get messages to the public, and because they do not have to be expensive "Madison Avenue" or well-polished ads to be effective, we should use them more often. Low-budget ads can be influential--that is, if done right. There are basically two kinds of ads: 1) live copy for straight narration by radio disc jockeys, and 2) pre-recorded tapes of one or two voices with music or other interesting sound effects. The advertiser's or Sandman's model can be used to design the latter. For example, put slides on video tape or film or get fancy by using slides to dissolve one image into another. There is lots of room for creativity in doing inexpensive ads. It is beyond the capability of this manual to give detailed directions on how to create and design effective low-budget ads, but below are some helpful points to consider before embarking upon such a venture:

1) Get local educational institutions to enter a contest for the best PSA. Classes can write and produce ads, with the winners getting their ads on T.V.

2) Build ongoing relations with local radio and T.V. station personnel so they will look forward to working with you on ads. Ask them for pointers. They might be helpful.

3) Get prestigious people to participate in ads or lend support. They do not have to be nationally known people; local celebrities will do well.

4) Consult retired radio or T.V. people for help on producing an ad.

5) Stations have their own public service policies and standards. Contact public service directors in your area to find out about such policies in order to take advantage of them.

To be eligible for PSAs, you must represent a nonprofit organization. To get PSAs aired, you: 1) cannot have advertising funds available for paid media, 2) must adhere to nonpolitical statements, and 3) should have some credability with the station manager.

Designing an Ad

Based upon the above information, each group should pick an issue and design an ad, keyed to the following:

1) Who would you contact for help in your community to design the ad? Are there local college or retired radio and T.V. people that could help with this? How would you find out about available resources in your community? Brainstorm a list of people or organizations that might be helpful.

2) What are the objectives of your PSA? Objectives help clarify what needs to be done. They provide the benchmarks to help make optimal decisions about time and money. Objectives provide criteria for performance evaluation. Now, what would a time line look like for getting a PSA done?

3) Some find it useful to get the audience to respond to PSAs by giving them a post office box. What reward could you give that's relatively inexpensive to encourage your audience to respond to your PSA? The response rate could be a way of evaluating the effectiveness of PSAs. Be creative.

4) How would you apply PSAs to the concept paper on *Media and Social and Environmental Change*?

News Releases

Another method of getting media coverage is to distribute news releases about your group's activities. A news release is planned news, written in a way so the editor will read and publish it. It has to be able to compete with other important news items for space. Following is a sample copy of a news release:

SAMPLE NEWS RELEASE

From: Susan Doe
For: The Midwest Environmental
     Action Group
     115 Steel Street
     Dayton, Ohio 02178
     (617) 855-1212

Subject: The Harmful Effects of Toxic Dumpsites

Date: March 25, 1983

FOR IMMEDIATE RELEASE

Are you bothered by the toxic and hazardous waste dumpsites that have been planned for this community? If so, The Harmful Effects of Toxic and Hazardous Waste Dumpsite--a New Community Menace is the topic of discussion at Huron High School, in Dayton, Tuesday, April 6, 8:00 p.m.

The Speaker is Dr. Barry Sears, former director of the Environmental Protection Agency and presently the director of an organization called People Against Toxic and Hazardous Waste, which has chapters located throughout the nation.

Dr. Sears has written several books and numerous articles on this subject. His most recent work is a book entitled *We Are Destroying Our Land and Our Health*.

Dr. Sears uses examples of how toxic and hazardous waste dumpsites can be harmful to our health. He will show where they can be found here in Ohio, and indicate what citizens groups can do to protect themselves.

For further information on the April 6th program, contact Susan Doe, 555-1212.

Press Conferences

Press conferences can also be an effective tool for media exposure. Social and environmental change has been successful in those communities that have been able to use effective TV coverage. The civil rights, peace, women's, ecology, and anti-nuclear movements have been successful in using such conferences. TV is the most powerful way to get one's point across, since large numbers of people watch it as opposed to reading the printed word.

Since many social issues are potentially explosive, we feel that groups or community organizations working on these issues should know about press conferences. Why have some been more successful than others in getting TV coverage? Why have some been more effective than others in getting their points across? Below are some hints which might prove to be useful:

1) Alert assignment editors; they decide what TV stories are to be covered and who will cover them. Often we talk to a political reporter; this is not the person to talk with if you want coverage. It's the assignment editor.

2) Have your press secretary or designate call the afternoon before the press conference or event, following with another call in the morning to stress the importance of your news.

3) Attempt to schedule your event between 10:00 a.m. and 2:30 p.m. on a weekday. Stations are usually short on personnel at night and on weekends, and would like to save their crews for emergencies. Your press conference or event must be finished by mid-afternoon, because it takes several hours to process and prepare the film for showing on the late afternoon and evening newscasts. Therefore, find a location as close to the TV station as possible, because assignment editors hate to waste crew time by having them travel to distant places.

4) Right from the beginning, keep both print and T.V. people informed about what's going on with respect to your issue. It's much better to prevent misunderstandings than to have to try to clear them up later.

5) If the media refuse to cover the event, do it yourself. Get school equipment, such as TV cameras and movie projectors, and students to help film your own press conference. Edit it to 80-second packages, attach a script, and ship it to TV stations.

6) Find out about the shift changes for crew members. It is less likely that they will respond if TV stations have to pay overtime to their crews. In addition, it will usually take 5 to 10 minutes for them to set up their cameras; do not hurry them. Remember they will be reaching about 80 percent of the people. Placate the print people by talking to them about political events or about some other topics. They do not like to wait for TV crews either.

7) Your statements should be short and simple. Have a prepared statement ready for the reporters, reading the part of the statement you want on TV. Read no more than two minutes of material. Include background information and facts to help reporters fill up their stories. The T.V. people will only use about 30 to 60 seconds. Break your key points into 20-second chunks separated by pauses; this helps the film editor.

8) The longer the press conference runs, the more likely the danger of the media people finding something that is unhelpful. Remember, you can control this by not saying that much and emphasizing only major themes. You may want to hand out written statements to print people near the end so that tough questions might be saved when there isn't much time.

9) Signal camera men when finished so they can film cutaways or transitions; then spend more time with the print people with respect to various unanswered questions.

10) Encourage community people to write editorials supporting a particular bill. Also, you may not want to get into a debate with the opposition. It may only inflame the situation. It really depends on the context and the issue.

11) Get a local paper to write a special-interest story on the environment--perhaps even a multi-part series.

Media Strategy

You are part of a community organization that has a media committee. (This is usually a luxury for most community organizations.) There are about six people on this committee. All are specialists in television, radio, brochures, and other printed materials. The committee has a role for a media coordinator. Members take turns functioning in this role. It is important to have a coordinator to oversee the entire media effort. Your community organization has decided to organize local people to stop the building of a nuclear power plant. This is a hot issue. As organizers, you were out talking with people about issues that affect their lives. They are deeply concerned about the building of a nuclear power plant in their community. You plan a big demonstration in about two months at the site where the nuclear power plant is to be built.

Pretend you are on the media committee of this organization:

1. What would be the media goals of this campaign?

2. Brainstorm a list of ideas/strategies for reaching each of the goals you mentioned.

3. Consult the Tactics and Skills Chart at the end of this manual. What tactics and skills would be most feasible for your group? Do you have the equipment? The skills? What will the outcome of your strategy be? How many people can you reach? How will the community react?

Session Number Nine: Communication

Objectives of the Session
To facilitate your analytical understanding of three communication models to be used for social change.

To provide opportunities for learning how to use media more effectively.

To provide opportunities for planning media strategies.

Design Flow in Minutes
5 minutes   Agenda review.
20 minutes   Compare the advantages and disadvantages of the communications models presented thus far.
30 minutes   Application of PSAs to Sandman's communication model. How would you apply it? (This is to be done in small groups.)

15 minutes   Break.
35 minutes   Share and critique each other's media strategies.
10 minutes   Evaluation.

Homework
Although the media is important for social and environmental change, it stills falls short of being truly effective with certain class-based groups. In working class neighborhoods, a combination of media and personal contact--or community organizing skills--will become important as citizens experience the effects of toxic dumpsites, polluted air and water, and the like. Read the concept paper on *Community Organizing* and the additional item on *Lobbying: Organizing to Influence Legislators*.

Concept Paper VI: Community Organizing

Community organizing is the intentional use of conflict and power to build strong community organizations to influence both corporate and governmental policies. Often community organizations will use conflict as a resource to interrupt ongoing routines of bureaucracies, and to gain power in order to make meaningful demands upon decision-makers. Without power there is little that community groups can do to make corporate managers or government incumbents respond to their needs. The art of power and compromise becomes important for community groups to win concessions from antagonists in order to attract people and financial resources to the organization.

The purpose of building organizations is to empower people to use social conflict and power as resources for SEC. The building of organizations is automatically perceived as an intrusion, which threatens existing power structures and institutional arrangements. It carries with it menacing implications of displacement and disorganization of the status quo. Empowering people through organization is not for a philanthropic or social service gesture; it is to build organizations to wield power to eradicate poverty, misery, delinquency, disease, injustice, hopelessness, and despair.

One example of a group involved in both teaching and community organizing is the Industrial Areas Foundation (IAF), located in Chicago and founded by Saul Alinsky. Much of the confrontational politics used by organizers has come from Alinsky's model. To be invited into a community, the IAF may request that the community raise two hundred thousand dollars or more to place in a local bank, giving their organizers signature power -- that is, the ability to sign checks and disburse money. This request is made for two basic reasons: 1) It tests the level of commitment of people asking for service; and 2) it is an organizing activity within itself.

While the IAF usually includes a number of representatives from community organizations, the IAF Board is responsible for turning out large numbers of people for an "action" or demonstration. The IAF is basically an organization of organizations, with a staff to help them research and articulate issues which appeal to self-interests of the community.

The Association for Community Organizations for Reform Now (ACORN), on the other hand, organizes individuals into neighborhood groups. These neighborhood groups in turn elect representatives to a city-wide board; the city elects to the state and the state to the national. Many of the organizing principles are the same as IAF.

Because the IAF style of community organizing, described in Alinsky's *Reveille for Radicals* (New York: Vintage Books, 1969), falls under the category of conflict I theory, it is a class strategy geared to changing conditions in local communities without confronting basic structural underpinnings in any meaningful way. However, there are organizers who support fundamental change within society or conflict II, but who find it is easier to raise issues and organize within the realm of what people find acceptable (conflict I). Unless under considerable stress or a crisis, most people find fundamental change unacceptable or act in ways that suggest their lack of interest. Yet it is possible, by working with people on a long-term basis or within crisis conditions, that they may come to embrace more basic societal change.

More Responsible

The conflict I focus is upon empowering community groups to make corporate and government decision-makers more responsible to their collective need within the context of our political economy. Often, such groups may organize themselves to obtain better lights in neighborhoods, get stop lights installed at dangerous intersections, get employers to hire more people from the local area, or get the city to increase its garbage collection. Some of these activities sound trivial, but they may be important in responding to local needs. Organizers should start where people are, in order to get them involved later in more substantive issues.

Because community groups often lack the necessary resources to enhance their power or because they seldom experience victory or a sense of self-determination, it is rather hard to get them involved in an activist mode. Organizers are to help people to help themselves and to build organizations that will be powerful and respected in the community. Also, organizers must be clear about personal motives. They must have a deeply felt sense of commitment to empower people for social justice.

While IAF organizers recognize that community groups lack both the power and authority to control forces affecting community life, they compensate for their lack of power (namely, wealth, connections, and institutional legitimacy) by depending upon social protest as a key resource for winning concessions from corporate and government agencies. Protests are only as effective as the ability of organizers and others to understand the complexity of hundreds of governmental bureaucracies and corporate structures (Bailey, 1974). Also, mass media, it is felt by some, is important if protests are to succeed, in that media widen the arena of conflict, thus giving organizations visibility and making potential supporters aware of issues. It encourages others to participate in building organizations in order to make them even stronger. Media exposure helps protests become an effective resource for social change. One picture may be worth more than 10,000 words.

Often protests are actions to interrupt daily routines of antagonist organizations. This necessitates class strategies that are creative, strategies that permit low-power groups with few, if any, political resources to obtain their goals. Therefore, a protest may be thought of as a form of social action directed at altering one or more policy goals by deliberate disruption or harassment to make local decision-makers or institutions more responsive to community needs, without seeking to destroy the political order of society.

It is important that organizers maintain contact with their constituency to keep them informed for organizational support. Contacting them through newsletters and public meetings to involve them in a variety of activities and organization-building events is critical for such support. The constituency is enlarged by having volunteers or paid canvassers go from door to door, both to ask for money, and to inform the public of all the "good things" the organization is doing.

Persuasion Theories and Community Organizing

Because much of organizing is contacting people individually, at least at the beginning stages, certain theories of persuasion are important for the organizer to understand and use when appropriate. While a whole body of literature on persuasion theory exists, community organizers have failed to make significant use of it. Even though much of this knowledge has been used to help maintain the status quo or to help corporations market their goods, there are some theories that can be used to enhance organizers' abilities to work more effectively with people. Ideas regarding social judgment and information integration are forwarded from Littlejohn (1983).

Social Judgment

Social judgment theory claims that people have a certain latitude of acceptance, rejection, and noncommitment to ideas and information. There is a range of statements, pro or con, that the person can tolerate; there is a range of statements that a person cannot tolerate; and there are statements that a person is uncommitted to or cares nothing about. Therefore, if information falls within one's latitude of acceptance or noncommitment, then we can expect that one's attitude will be easier to change than if such statements fall into one's latitude of rejection. This means that the more discrepant the message from the person's own stand, providing that it falls within his or her attitude of acceptance, the greater the expected attitude change.

Specifically, what does social judgment theory means for organizing? How can this theory be used? It basically means there are certain concepts, language, and ideas that fall into a person's latitude of rejection. Though well-intentioned, organizers who use Marxist language with certain constituencies may be appealing to the latitude of rejection of the people they are attempting to organize. Appealing to the latitude of rejection by using certain language will in all probability lead to failure in mobilizing a community group for certain desired ends. Yet, there are language and symbols within our culture that carry the same message which falls within the latitude of one's acceptance. Once I asked a class of about 200 students how many believed in socialism and only a few raised their hands. Then I asked how many believed in economic democracy and about 85 percent raised their hands. Obviously, it was the word democracy that fell into their latitude of acceptance. History is full of people we hold in high esteem who use a language of change and revolution that falls into one's latitude of acceptance. The task of the organizer is not only to find out the latitude of acceptance or rejection but to find, by looking to history for appropriate language, ways to work most effectively in organizing people. This does not mean that Marxist or leftist terminology cannot be used. It depends upon the latitude of acceptance or rejection of the people to be influenced.

Before we leave this theory, there is one other important factor that should be considered: ego involvement. Ego involvement is the degree to which one's attitude toward something affects the self-concept of the person. If the message is close to one's position and an important one, then it will be assimilated. Therefore, the greater one's ego involvement, the larger the latitude of rejection and the smaller the latitude of noncommitment and acceptance. Thus, we can expect little change in attitude. If, for instance, the person you are trying to involve in some collective action or organizational membership is already ego-involved with respect to the issue or the organization, you will undoubtedly not have to change this person's attitude, but direct the energy into constructive outlets. Yet, if a person is ego-involved with an issue that is contrary to the goals and mission of the organization, then obviously it will do little good to spend time convincing this person of your point of view, because the latitude of rejection is too large. That is to say, if the person is ego-involved with an issue, then, no matter what you say, your arguments will in all probability be rejected.

Information Integration

Another theory of persuasion that can be applied to community organizing is information integration. The degree to which information will affect attitudes depends upon two variables: 1) valence and 2) weight. Valence, the degree to which the information is good or bad, will determine the degree of acceptance or integration of that information by the individual. Information that supports one's beliefs is generally viewed as good news, and information opposing as bad news. Weight is the importance that is assigned to the information. If the person thinks the information is true, then a higher weight is assigned to the information than otherwise.

How does information integration relate to community organizing? How can it be used? Presenting an individual with an opportunity to join an organization that will cham-

pion an issue may be good news. While the information may be good news, it is only half the battle. The other half is feeling that the information is true or believable. This will undoubtedly place a considerable amount of pressure on the organizer to be convincing. The ability to change a person's attitude will also depend upon personal appearance and interpersonal skills.

Strategy I: Dialogue and Self-Interests

Often working class people, like others, understand events in the realm of their own experience. Organizers from middle-class backgrounds need to be sensitive to people's experiences for effective dialogue with them. Dialogue beyond their experience increases social distance, preventing organizer effectiveness. If organizers cannot find points in the experience to which people can relate, then organizers must create that experience. (Remember, there are important differences between talking to people and carrying on dialogue.) Sometimes this is done by using analogies. In short, communication is a major part of organizing. If one cannot communicate effectively, then it will be rather difficult to organize people. In the example below, Alinsky, the noted community organizer, speaks to problems of communicating with people:

This is the problem in trying to communicate on the issue of the H bomb. It is too big. It involves too many casualties. It is beyond the experience of people and they just react with "Yeah, it is a terrible thing," but it really doesn't grip them. It is the same thing with figures. The moment one gets into the area of $25 million and above, let alone a billion, the listener is completely out of touch, no longer really interested, because the figures have gone above his experience and almost are meaningless. Millions of Americans do not know how many million dollars make up billion (Alinsky, 1972).

Dialogue is important because it helps us to understand a variety of self-interests. Self-interests are preferences based upon our sense of who we are and what we feel is important for our own needs, aspirations, values, goals, and survival. Self-interest is a learned cultural phenomenon that indicates to us what is proper and highly valued. It could be independence, individuality, personal gain, need for love, security, creativity, rest, separateness, self-esteem, or self-respect. In other instances, self-interest is related to a more basic level of survival, such as having enough to eat, a decent place to stay, enough warmth for comfort, and physical security.

Although self-interest can be destructive, particularly if it's defined too narrowly or if people fail to be considerate of others, it can be used for constructive purposes. People seldom come together for collective action out of a sense of moral purpose, but out of self-interest. Self-interest provides the energy and motivation that lead to collective action. The organizer needs to be a good listener to identify critical self-interests.

For example, the local minister wants to join the organization because high crime encourages church members to migrate to the suburbs. The local grocery store owner is concerned due to large numbers of burglaries he has had over the last year. Senior citizens are interested because large numbers of social security checks are stolen from mail boxes. Homeowners are interested in getting boarded-up homes demolished, because they become havens for derelicts and dope parties. Others perceive this as a chance to be part of an organization to exert leadership influence in the community. People come together out of their own interests, providing the fuel to propel the group into action. People come together out of threats to physical security, economic loss, and a need for a self-esteem.

Olson (1971), however, has challenged the assumption that individuals join organizations or operate in behalf of their self-interests. Unless individuals are in a group that is quite small, unless they are in some way coerced, or unless there is some other device to make individuals act in their rational self-interest, individuals will not act to achieve their common or group interests. For instance, if I stand to benefit from the collection of others, then why should I join them? Why shouldn't I let the others do the work for me? In this way, it costs me nothing, and I stand to gain tremendously. This kind of person is known as the free rider.

Olson goes on to say that one way of getting around this is by selective incentives. Giving individuals an incentive will increase the number of participants. Prairiefire, a farm organization which is a part of the Iowa Farm Unity Coalition, has thought about designing a farmer insurance program that will undersell insurance offered through the Farm Bureau, all in order to attract members away from them and to build a stronger Farm Unity Coalition or a stronger Prairiefire. In some instances, it is most appropriate to use selective incentives to build organizations. It may be that in rural organizing, in particular, where people live far apart and find it difficult to get together, that some sort of selective incentive will work to help increase both their interests and participation. In other instances, solidarity, outside threats to a group, or the importance of an issue may be enough to organize around self-interests. But the heart of the matter is that we should not waste time on debating the numbers issue. It only takes a small percentage to bring about social change, as evidenced by the social movements in this country and revolutions throughout the world.

Strategy II: Victories

Victories are, indeed, important in building organizations. Often people are a part of organizations experiencing little success. Therefore, it becomes critical that protests--the major resource for policy changes--result in victories that people feel good about. It is important that organizations in their infancy do not take on an issue that is not winnable. A loss will set the organization back several months. Even if the organization fails to win, it is important to talk about the event as if it were a victory. Thus, it is important that issues be carefully framed to ensure success. An example of a success story is the Community Organization for Public Service (COPS):

> The story of COPS is a rare success story. It is the story of a group which has not only survived, but has won fights and moved on to new, often more difficult, struggles. The group began by tackling the most nitty gritty of environmental problems----the poor drainage on San Antonio's Mexican-American west and south sides. But in six years, the organization has taken on poor schools, inadequate health care, rising utility rates, and pollution. Through its efforts, COPS claims, some $300 million in government funds have been channeled into old neighborhoods, financing projects which now dot the south and west sides----and to a lesser extent the black east side: drainage systems, new pavement, sidewalks, parks, libraries, new homes and rehabilitated old ones (Robinson, 1980).

The paragraph above demonstrates how a community organization was able to start out with relatively small victories, leading to larger ones. It is interesting to note that many of the issues they took on were environmental ones. The hard rains turned streets into rivers, with puddles lingering for days. When the local cement plant wanted to convert from a gas to a coal-fired generating plant, the local community became concerned about the sulfur dioxide, nitrous oxides, and particulate matter that would result from such a change and organized against it.

COPS' effectiveness came from the use of a variety of strategies. In addition to making public the cement company's campaign contributions to local politicians, sixty people from COPS went to the state capital in Austin to meet with the Texas Air Pollution Control Board, obtaining a second hearing on the cement company's application to burn coal. Also, after one heavy rain, 500 people confronted the city manager on drainage problems. They gathered signatures on petitions to influence zoning decisions. They held accountability nights for candidates to listen and respond to COPS concerns. These are only a few strategies used by COPS to get corporate power and government to change their policies.

Strategy III: Multiple Issues

A community organization can be geared to take on multiple issues similar to what COPS did in Texas. Multiple issues keep energies flowing with organizations by keeping a variety of people involved; they provide multiple reasons for organizations to exist. Once an issue is solved or has peaked, then another issue moves to the forefront, bringing with it a whole new set of community actors. For example, the weakness of a single issue organization is that once it accomplishes its goal or mission, there is no reason left for it to exist. The anti-nuclear movement has found it difficult to redirect itself to other goals now that nuclear power plants are in less demand by utility companies. The nuclear freeze floundered as a result of its success. Multiple issues have brought stability to organizations.

As the welfare state grows, people become more reliant upon governments to deliver certain goods and services. People look to the future for retirement on their social security, and plan their lives accordingly. The state administers unemployment insurance to temporarily protect workers against want and need. A number of welfare programs are designed to help the less fortunate or to provide them with income until they regain their earning power. The role of government in the lives of people has expanded.

The need for organizations in communities is just as important as the need for unions in the work place. The proliferation of community organizations and neighborhood groups in past decades indicates they serve important intermediary functions to bridge the gap between citizens and the government at all levels.

Tactics and Skills

The chart on community organizing at the end of this volume brings together the tactics and skills that we have been discussing throughout the manual. It provides a context in which we can organize our thoughts regarding a change process that is dependent upon conflict and power. In the initial stages, there should be a formulation of a change unit that has specific concerns or objectives.

The chart gives an idea of the various phases and stages of a campaign involved in community organizing. Study it carefully and then move on to the article on lobbying.

The information-gathering stage is not only to collect information for diagnostic purposes, but it is used as a basis for determining action tactics, skills, and strategies. It is also a way of letting others know that there are people concerned about these issues and of identifying potential support for change activities.

A part of the action strategy is to take this information and frame it in such a way that it appeals to the self-interests of those you are trying to organize. Such strategies take considerable amounts of creativity to be successful.

Following the strategy session, the change unit should mobilize public support for action or strategy. A number of ways of obtaining support are through membership lists, other organizations that might be interested in the issues, press conferences, flyers, public announcements, etc.

The actual showdown is a contest of strength and power. Often it is a time when the change unit gets the antagonist to recognize it as a legitimate negotiating body. Or they get the antagonist to make concessions. As mentioned before, victories or concessions from antagonists are important in building an organization.

While the evaluation process is to determine how effective the action has been, it is also a time to assess the victories that are to be publicized. Building an organization is based upon winning victories so that antagonists will recognize the organization as a power broker, consultant, or negotiator. People seldom like to be a part of a losing organization. If, however, the change unit has not been successful, then it returns back to the diagnostic stage and the process begins over again.

When there are tangible victories, the last stage consists of monitoring. One has to monitor to make sure that agreements are not violated. This stage should also consist of a mechanism by which questions regarding the violation of agreements can be raised and dealt with constructively. If no mechanism exists, and if violations occur, then in all likelihood the change unit will have to start the showdown all over again. The monitoring stage is definitely an important one.

While the chart of the change model shows general steps in the change process, the time line is more specific. The time line helps organizers think in more specific terms of what needs to be done for the mobilization of resources for a particular action goal or showdown. In the strategy and tactics phase, the force field analysis may be used to help organizers clarify strategies and tactics that may be appropriate for the situation. In addition, organizers may get an idea of various tactics and strategies to use in a given situation by referring to the tactics and skills chart.

Lobbying: Organizing to Influence Legislators

Basically the same principles used in community organizing are used to influence legislators. Keep in mind that building an organization or a constituency is the focus of organizing to influence a legislator. A review of the section on community organizing may be helpful at this point. But why is organizing important to influence legislators? It is important because senators and Representatives are sensitive to organized opinion, particularly if there is broad-based support for it. They want to be responsive to their constituency in order to be re-elected.

It is important for people to speak at public hearings with the presence of large numbers of members showing their support. Participation and victory are important to attract potential members, making issues known to the larger aggregate.

Some important points to remember as a lobbyist:

1) Get appointments by calling legislators' field offices to see them on their next scheduled trip home, or call their secretaries in the state capital.

2) If legislators ask a lot of hostile questions, do not assume they are against you. If they are on your side, give them support; make them feel good about supporting your issue so they will work harder for your goals.

3) If you cannot see legislators in person, then see their staff. Legislative staff people can be very helpful.

4) Being hostile or late for appointments, or talking too much, makes a bad impression. You will not influence them in this way. They are very busy people and often feel resentful if thrown off their schedules.

5) Present yourself first by telling them how they can be helpful. For instance: "I think the toxic waste bill deserves your support and I'd like to tell you why..." List no more than three points. Be concise and stay within five minutes. Then ask: "Can I count on your support?" You are entitled to know if they will support your bill.

6) Make sure your facts are accurate or you will lose credibility. It is very important to give accurate information.

7) Have a letter-writing party to get people to send of letters to legislators in support of your bill. Letters can be based upon the same theme, but each should be different.

8) Specific goals and timelines are important and should be adhered to in order to accomplish your work. Timelines help people to be accountable to one another.

Session Number Ten: An Assessment

Objectives of the Session

To familiarize you with the basic principles of community organizing.

To provide opportunities for you to assess your own skills for social change.

Design Flow in Minutes

5 minutes   Agenda review.

35 minutes   Pick an issue and organize a campaign around it based on the concept paper on *Community Organizing* and the tactics and skills chart.

15 minutes   Report information discussed in small groups.

10 minutes   Break.

10 minutes   Resource Assessment Chart (fill out and divide into threes and discuss).

35 minutes   Discussion of Resource Assessment Chart in total group.

10 minutes   Final evaluation.

Tactics and Skills

While it is often difficult to discern the difference between strategy and tactics, we should nonetheless attempt to do so. What makes it so difficult is that one person's strategy is another person's tactic. In this manual, strategies are viewed as being more general or abstract. For example, appealing to people's self-interests to get them to support and take a more active role in the organization is a strategy. To take on issues that are winnable and to intentionally celebrate those victories as a means of building an organization are strategies. Activities with the intention of empowering people or the organization to which they belong are strategies. There are other strategies, too. While strategies are similar to overall goals, tactics are more specific and similar to objectives. They are specific and highly calculated behaviors which support

overall strategies. For example, a strategy might be to build a powerful organization that can win concessions from antagonists. But a tactic might be to get people to withhold payment of their utility bills to force the utility company to lower its rates. Such a victory will make the organization more attractive for people to join, which in turn increases its power. Skills, on the other hand, may be thought of as how well we plan and carry out strategies and tactics.

While social protests may be a strategy based upon symbolic activity, seeking to dramatize to the community the need for change by appealing to their consciousness, it does have its shortcomings. It does not control the meaning which the community may give to the protest activity. While the picketers may be protesting an injustice of some kind, the community may view them as basically troublemakers. Nonetheless, it can be a powerful strategy for facilitating social change. Resistance is another social change strategy. It attempts to facilitate change by interfering with the ongoing operations of an institution and thereby forcing a serious response from antagonists. The antagonists must, however, concede to permitting change, or it must use force in sufficient measure to break the resistance. And while rebellion, another social change strategy, is an extension of resistance, it seeks to use force to gain control of the situation and its resources. Protest, resistance, and rebellion can take many forms; many tactics can be used to enhance the effectiveness of these strategies.

Even though the reader might disagree with both the criteria and the analysis of the various tactics, the purpose of this chart is to get the reader to combine a number of tactics based upon their potential for effectiveness. Tactics and strategies should not be taken lightly; they should be debated and altered, if deemed necessary.

Now use the chart beginning on the next page as a basis for making a time line for social change. Consult the tactics and skills chart for information to be used on your timeline.

Appendix One:

Tactics, Skills and Risk Assessment Charts

On the following eight pages are a *Tactics and Skills Chart*, which provides an in-depth view of the various steps available for Social and Environmental Change, and a *Risk Assessment Chart*, for use in evaluating such steps.

TACTICS AND SKILLS CHART

	Expertise, Level of Skill	Potential Scope of Influence	Kind of Power	Personal Risk	Organization Building	Strengths	Limitations
Press Release	Writer (high)	low/mod	Expert Referent	low	low	Free publicity reaches large numbers of people	May not be good for reaching target audience and limits selection of time of day, page it appears on, size of article (which determines notice)
PSAs	Public Rel. (high)	mod	Expert Referent	low	low	Free, good for educating. Can be done cheaply. Potential of reaching large numbers of people	Aired at odd hours with little likelihood that it will be noticed
Interview Shows	Knowledgable Person (high)	high	Expert Referent	low	low	Free publicity allowing time to educate and clarify issue. Allows org. to speak for self. May reach large numbers	Limited audience, usually inexpensively produced. People may tune out after a short time
Columns & Feature Stories	Writer (mod/high)	high	Expert Referent	low	low	Attracts attention, more space used to get across issues	Limited audience
Posters (mod)	Artists	low	Referent	low	low	Visual presentation to publicize an event	Need time for postering. Art work can be expensive. Posters may be short-lived, in that people tear them down. City ordinance might limit where you can post
Slide Shows	Editor (mod/high)	low	Expert Referent	low	low	Visual stimulation and narrative informs audience about issues	If elaborate, can be expensive. Includes shooting pictures and editing

TACTICS AND SKILLS CHART (continued)

	Expertise, Level of Skill	Potential Scope of Influence	Kind of Power	Personal Risk	Organization Building	Strengths	Limitations
Newsletter	Editor (high)	mod	Expert Referent	low	mod	Good for networking and dissemination of in-depth information. Provides forum for community people, may act as a clearinghouse	Costly, time-consuming, needs supplies and printing capability
Propaganda	Propagandist (high)	high	Expert Referent	low	mod	Reaches large numbers of people. Uses multiple means for getting messages out to people	People suspicious of propaganda, associated with war effort
Brochures	Editor (high)	low/mod	Expert Referent	low	mod	Means for publicizing the organization and its goal in moderate detail	Limited circulation, may be expensive to mail and/or time consuming to deliver door-to-door
Rallies	Organizers (low)	low	Expert Legitimate	low	high	Informs people of issue, creates feeling of solidarity, attracts attention of passers-by	Often fails to lead to follow-up actions, reaches limited number of people, may attract counter-demonstrations or rallies
Fund-raising	Grant Writers Strategic (high)	mod/high	Referent Legitimate Reward	low/high	mod	Basic ingredient is keeping organizations afloat, provides opportunities, more organizational options	Too much money too fast may cause org. problems related to rapid growth
Door Knocking	Organizers (mod)	low	Referent Reward Coerc.	low/mod	mod	Face-to-face contact exposing people to issues, high influence situation	Tedious process, limited in the number of people reached

TACTICS AND SKILLS CHART (continued)

	Expertise, Level of Skill	Potential Scope of Influence	Kind of Power	Personal Risk	Organization Building	Strengths	Limitations
Opinion Leaders	Organizers (mod/high)	low/mod	Referent	low	mod	Face-to-face contact of opinion leaders with opinion followers. High influence situation	Limited in number of people reached
Art	Artists (mod/high)	low	Reward	low	low	Visual stimulation, good for consciousness raising	Little art accessible to low power groups
Action Research	Research-ers (high)	low	Expert Coerc.	low	mod/high	Type of information gathered lends itself to organizing and organization building. Creates feeling of empowerment	Tedious hours of detailed work which may be costly
Academic Research	Research-ers (high)	low/mod	Expert	low	mod/high	Highly credible free use of information in the public domain	Often doesn't lend itself to organizing, too abstract
Investi-gative Report	Reporters (high)	low/mod	Expert Coerc.	low	mod/high	Broad dissemination of information of wrong-doing	No follow-up to organizing or organization building. Assumes readers will automatically do the right thing to correct the situation
Petition Drive	Organizers (mod)	low	Legitimate	low	mod/high	Fact-to-face contacts. Influential for getting people to make behavioral commitments. Names and addresses can be used for follow-up activity. Good organizational tool	Reaches limited number of people. Takes considerable time

TACTICS AND SKILLS CHART (continued)

	Expertise, Level of Skill	Potential Scope of Influence	Kind of Power	Personal Risk	Organi- zation Building	Strengths	Limitations
Whistle Blowing	Low alien- ated and disaf- fected workers (mod)	mod/high	Expert Coerc.	high	low/mod	Opportunities to make known public corp. or government wrong-doing	Personal and professional threats with loss of job. Scapegoated, professional isolation, hard on family
Lobbying	Lobbyists (mod/high)	mod/high	Expert Coerc.	low	mod/high	Fact-to-face contact. Influential with legislators, who are vulnerable to outside pressures	Could be costly in terms of time, competition with other highly fianced lobbyists
Political Campaign	Money Campaign Mgrs. (high)	mod/high	Legitimate Reward Referent Coerc.	low	low/high	Combines multiple skills and strategies to inform and influence voting behavior	Expensive, difficult to get people out to vote. Voting made difficult by inconvenient voter registration. Distrust of the political system
Media & Attitude Change	Media person (high)	mod/high	Reward Referent	low	mod	Reaches large numbers of people, visual presen- tation of issues	Costly, content edited, limited time and space
Direct Non- violence	Organizers (high)	low/mod	Reward Referent Coerc.	high	mod/high	Provides opportunities for people to become directly involved acting upon their behavioral commitments. Builds solidarity	Potential risk of bodily harm, depending on issue. Demon- strators may not be firmly committed to nonviolence, increasing chances for retali- ation or violence if attacked
Conflict Negotiations	Negoti- ators (high)	mod/high	Reward Coerc. Expert	high	mod/high	Ariculates issue, providing opportunities for creative solutions	Attempts to negotiate from position of unequal power, disadvantaging one in outcome solutions

TACTICS AND SKILLS CHART (continued)

	Expertise, Level of Skill	Potential Scope of Influence	Kind of Power	Personal Risk	Organization Building	Strengths	Limitations
Guerilla Theater	Production Mgrs. (mod/high)	low	Referent Expert	low	low	Visual attention to issue. Use of humans	Limited audience, doesn't lead to follow-up activities
Speak Out	Speakers (high)	low	Referent Expert	low/high	low/mod	Credible speakers can have impact if uses both emotional appeal and facts	Scope of influence limited to small audiences. Low interaction between speaker and audience. May not be follow-up activities
Teach-in	Organizers Money (mod/high)	low	Expert Referent	low	mod	Credible speakers can have impact if uses both emotional appeal and facts	Scope of influence limited. Often not clear on strategies or next steps
Personal Support System	Friends (low/mod)	low	Referent Reward	low	mod/high	Provides renewed energy, confidence, self-affirmation to continue struggle	Overdependence prevents action on part of individual
Large Group Facilitation	Leadership (high)	low	Referent Expert Reward	low	low/high	Often used to provide structure and efficiency to decisionmaking	Unfamiliarity produces chaos and inefficiency, or a knowledgeable few can control meetings
Small Group Meeting	Group Facilitators (high)	low	Referent Expert	low	low/high	Maximal participation for problem solving and strategizing	Unskilled participants or highly emotional issue may bog members down in conflict
Evaluation	Evaluators (high)	low/mod	Expert	low	low/high	Provides yardstick for measuring goals, giving feedback and direction that should be taken	In an action organization, the evaluation is secondary or less than important. Sometimes expensive

TACTICS AND SKILLS CHART (continued)

	Expertise, Level of Skill	Potential Scope of Influence	Kind of Power	Personal Risk	Organization Building	Strengths	Limitations
Public Hearings	Organizer (high)	mod	Expert Referent	low	low/high	Informs decision-makers and participants. Keeps issue before the public. Good for presenting facts, personal stories, can be staged for maximal impact	May be difficult for working people to attend, problems of babysitters
Training	Trainers (high)	mod/high	Expert	low	high	Increases skill levels of participants	Takes time, can be costly
Pilgrimage	Organizers (high)	low	Referent Coerc. Reward	high	high	Opportunities for direct participation acting on behavioral commitment. Attracts passers-by	Scope of influence limited
Non-cooperation, withdrawal, withholding, lockouts, strikes, and disobedience	Organizers Money (high)	low/mod	Coerc. (disruptive)	low/mod	mod	May disrupt ongoing operations, costing antagonist money or organizational pride	May be dangerous, depending on situation
Fast	Organizers, Committee People (low/high)	low/mod	Coerc. (moral conscience)	low/high	mod	Articulates issue to widen area for additional support. Appeal to moral fiber or consciousness of wider public	Has to be done in conjunction with an effective media strategy. Risk health and may result in death. May cost antagonist money
Alternative Institutions	Business Mgt. (high)	mod	Referent (mod)	high	mod	Models of what can be, with respect to social relations in the workplace and community	Odds against the success of small business and alternative institutions

TACTICS AND SKILLS CHART (continued)

	Expertise level of skill	Potential Scope of Influence	Kind of Power	Personal Risk	Organization Building	Strengths	Limitations
Mock Awards & Mock Elections	Organizers (mod)	low	Coerc. (embarrassment)	low	high	Use of humor to inform. Builds solidarity	Audience might misinterpret. Scope of influence limited
Symbolic Acts	Organizers (mod)	low	Coerc.	low	high	Use to attach significance to issue. People influenced by symbols	Scope of influence limited
Vigils	Organizers (mod)	low	Coerc.	low	high	Symbols can be used to inform	Scope of influence limited
Singing	Organizers (mod/high)	low	Reward	low	high	Builds solidarity. Educates people about history and struggles	Scope of influence limited to participants

	Risk Assessment Chart		
	Fully Developed and Available	Partially Developed but Not Available	Not Developed
A part of an affinity group or close network of friends			
Ideology clarity regarding social change			
Fin. security to allow you to work for meager wages			
Energy: physical & emotional			
Willing to take risks (Social status/role)			
Expertise in some area/ academic discipline			
Macro and micro diagnostic skills			
Long–range planning activities			
Organizing others like yourself			
Organizing people in the streets"			
Confronting enemies/ opponents			
Public speaking skills			
Management of organizations			
Personal style adaptive to change			
Ability to self-direct growth			

Appendix Two:
Financial Definitions

Accounting Equation: Assets=Liabilities+Owners' Equity (A=L+OE). Always state assets, liabilities and owners' equity in monetary terms.

Accounts Payable: A company's debts to suppliers of goods or services.

Accounts Receivable: Amounts due to a firm from customers.

Accrued Expenses Payable: Obligations such as wages and salaries, interest on borrowed funds, and pensions.

Asset: Resources of value to the firm (a service potential or the ability to provide service to its owner); must have a measurable cost to the firm which becomes the monetary value of the asset.

Balance Sheet: Statement of assets, liabilities and owners' (stockholders) equity at any point in time (i.e., A=L+OE).

Bond: Agreement to pay a specified sum (called the "principal") either at a future date or periodically over the course of a loan, during which time a fixed rate of interest may be paid on certain dates. Bonds are issued by corporations, and by federal, state, and local governments. They are typically used for long-term financing.

Break-Even Point: Level of output at which a firm's total revenue equals its total cost (or its average revenue equals its average total costs), so that its net revenue is zero. At a break-even point, as defined in economics, a firm is normally profitable, since total cost in economics includes nor-mal profit.

Budget : Itemized estimate of expected revenues and expenditures for a given period in the future.

Capital: 1) As a factor of production, capital is produced by means of further production (such as capital goods or investment goods in the form of raw materials, machines, or equipment) for the ultimate purpose of manufacturing consumer goods. Hence, human resources are also part of an economy's capital..

2) As money, capital represents the funds which businesspersons use to purchase capital goods.

Capital Market: Center where long-term credit and equity instruments such as bonds, stocks, and mortgages are bought and sold.

Capital Stock: Unit of ownership in a corporation; it represents the stockholder's proprietary interest. Two major classes are common stock and preferred stock.

Compound Interest: Interest computed on a principal sum and also on all the interest earned by the principal sum as of a given date.

Consumer Price Index (CPI): Average of prices of goods and services commonly purchased by families in given geographical areas. Generally referred to as a "cost-of-living index," the CPI is published by the Bureau of Labor Statistics of the U.S. Department of Labor.

Current Assets: Expect to convert to cash within one year.

Current Liabilities: Due to be paid within one year.

Disinvestment: Reduction in the total stock of capital goods caused by failure to replace it as it wears out. Example: the consumption or using up of factories, machines, etc., at a faster rate than they are being replaced so that the production base is diminishing.

Double Taxation: The taxing of both the company and dividends.

Dividends: Unearned income, taking equity out of company and paying it to stockholders.

Enterprise: Collection of assets subject to common control and employed for profit.

Expense (according to an accountant): Asset consumed in pursuit of income during the period. Measured by historical cost.

Expense (according to an economist): Decrease in value of assets.

FIFO: Method of inventory. Will show high earnings on the inventory that is "First In and First Out." Balance sheet will show higher profits. Company pays higher taxes.

Fixed Assets: Land, plant equipment, etc. Assumes an ongoing factory or business, hence these items will not be liquidated within one year. Order of liquidity normally determines location on balance sheet -- more current first.

General Journal: Book of original entry. As the source documents are processed, and their impact ascertained, they are recorded in the General Journal.

General Ledger: Listing of all accounts and balances; namely, detailed listing of all asset, liability, and owners' equity accounts, including all revenue and expense accounts. From the journal, amounts are posted in ledger in appropriate accounts.

Income Statement (Profit and Loss Statement): Listing the income change in net assets during any specific period of time caused by profit-oriented activity of the enterprise.

Intangible Assets (Assets which have value but are not physically observable): They include such things as patents (right to use specific processes), options (right to purchase another asset), and goodwill (value of earning power).

Liabilities and Owners' Equity: Claims by creditors and owners on assets of firm (Assets financed from two sources: 1) creditors [outsiders]: accounts payable, notes payable, etc., and 2) owners [insiders]: owner's equity, proprietorship, etc.) Liabilities and Owners' Equity represents claims on assets of enterprise by creditors and stockholders, respectively.

Liquidity: Ease with which an asset can be converted into cash quickly, without loss of value in terms of money. Liquidity is thus a matter of degree. Money is perfectly liquid, whereas any other asset possesses a lower degree of liquidity -- depending on conditions.

Long Term Debt: Amounts invested or reinvested in the firm by owners.

Loss: Net assets decrease as a result of

profit-oriented activity.

LIFO: Method of inventory, "Last In, First Out." Company will show lower profit. Company pays lower tax.

Market Price: Actual price that prevails in a market at any particular moment.

Merger: Amalgamation of two or more firms under one ownership. The three common forms are: 1) horizontal, uniting similar plants and products; 2) vertical, uniting dissimilar plants in various stages of production of similar products; and 3) conglomerate, uniting dissimilar plants and products.

Monopoly: Industry or market structure characterized by a single firm producing a product for which there are no close substitutes. The firm thus constitutes the entire industry and is a "pure" monopoly.

Net Assets: Assets minus Liabilities equals Owner's Equity.

Net-Profit Ratio: Ratio of a firm's net profit after taxes to its net sales. It is one of several general measures of a company's performance.

Net Worth: Difference between the total assets or things of value owned by a firm or individual, and the liabilities or debts that are owed.

Net Working Capital: Current Assets minus Current Liabilities.

Owner's Equity: Difference between assets and liabilities.

Payback: Measures the number of years required to recoup an investment.

Preferred Stock: Shares of stock that receive priority (i.e., preference) over common stock at a fixed rate in the distribution of dividends, or in the distribution of assets if the company is liquidated.

Prepayments: Business expenditures made in advance for items that will yield portions of their benefits in the present and in future years. Examples: advance premiums on a fire insurance policy, expenses incurred in marketing a new product.

Profit: Net assets increase as a result of profit-oriented

activity.

Promissory note: Commitment by one person to pay another a specified sum of money by a given date, usually within a year.

Residual Profit: Revenue minus expenses equals profit.

Revenue (according to an accountant): Gross inflow of assets arising from the firm's performance of productive services for outside customers or clients.

Revenue (according to an economist): Gross increase in value of assets.

Source Documents: Purchase invoice, warehouse receipt, interest notice, etc. As this information is brought to the attention of the person(s) responsible for processing such data, the documents must be analyzed in terms of the impact upon assets, liabilities, and owner's equity.

Straight Line Depreciation: Depreciation by a fixed amount over a fixed period of time.

Surtax: Imposed on a tax base in addition to a so-called normal tax. Example: A surtax on income in addition to the normal income tax. Note that a surtax is imposed on an existing tax base; it is not a "tax on a tax" as is popularly believed.

Tangible Assets: Assets whose existence is observable. Includes auto and transportation services, cash and ability to purchase goods and/or services, equipment, such as manufactured goods and clear land.

Weighted Average Method: Method of inventory. An average between LIFO and FIFO method.

Appendix Three:
Additional Sources of Information

Michigan Association of Counties
319 W. Lenawee St.
Lansing, MI 48933
(517) 372-5374
This office can help you locate other offices you are looking for and give detailed information on them. State associations are likely to know how to contact the county governments within their area. They can be very helpful. Most states have this kind of association.

Freedom of Information Reading Room
Internal Revenue Service
1111 Constitution Ave. NW
Washington, DC 20224
(202) 566-3770
You can get a copy of tax returns on nonprofit corporations. Nonprofit corporations are required to file Form 990 with the Internal Revenue Service. Information includes gross sales and receipts, total assets and liabilities, net worth, amount spent for political purposes, name of accountant, names and salaries of officers, directors, and trustees, fees paid for fund-raising, cash, securities, and land owned.

Bar Association of Washington, D.C.
1819 H St. NW, Suite 300
Washington, DC 20036
(202) 223-1484
Contact this office and they will give you information on where to apply to get information under the Freedom of Information Act.

Washington Researchers
918 16th Street, NW
Washington, DC 20006
(202) 828-4800
Much of the information in this manual came from this group. They have a more comprehensive book called *How to Find Information About Companies*. They can be helpful to you in learning the court system, how to use investigative services, credit reporting and bond rating services, information services, and data base services. They are helpful in other areas as well.

The Renegotiation Board
2000 M St. NW
Washington, DC 20446
(202) 254-8266
Reviews of contracts worth more than $1 million with government agencies. The board searches for excess profits. Will copy for 15 cents per page.

Public Information Reference Unit
Environmental Protection Agency
401 M St. SW, Room 2404 (PM213)
Washington, DC 20460
(202) 755-2808
Comments on EPA-proposed legislation, Environmental Impact Statements and EPA comments on the statements, state environmental plans and EPA guidelines. (Copying: first 25 pages free; 10 cents per page in excess of 25. Copying must be done by 4:15 p.m. and only checks are accepted, no cash).

Energy Information Administration Clearinghouse
Department of Energy
1726 M St., NW, Room 200
Washington, DC 20461
(202) 634-5610
Statistical information describing production and consumption related to energy. Some publications are free. A free brochure is available describing the publications.

Public Information Office
Occupational Safety and Health Review Commission
1825 K St. NW, Room 701
Washington, DC 20006
(202) 634-7943
Case transcripts and decisions concerning safety and health problems at any company which has employees and is involved in interstate commerce. This commission rules on disputes arising from inspections by the Occupational Safety and Health Administration.

Appendix Four:
Bibliography

Community Organizing

Belden, J., Edwards, G., Guyer, C. and Webb, L. (eds.) *New Directions in Farm, Land and Food Policies: A time for State and Local Action.* Agriculture Project, Conference on Alternative State and Local Policies, 1901 Que Street, N.W., Washington, DC 20009.

Biagi, Bob. *Working Together: A Manual for Helping Groups Work More Effectively.* University of Mass. (Citizen Involvement Training Project), 1978.

Dale, D. and Mitiguy, Nancy. *Planning for a Change: A Citizen's Guide to Creative Planning and Program Development.* University of Mass. (Citizen Involvement Training Project), 1978.

Dale, Duane. *Beyond Experts: A Guide for Citizen Group Training.* University of Massachusetts (Citizen Involvement Training Project), 1978.

Dale, Duane. *How to Make Citizen Involvement Work: Strategies for Developing Clout..* University of Mass. (Citizen Involvement Training Project), 1978.

Speeter, Greg. *Power: A Repossession Manual.* University of Mass. (Citizen Involvement Training Project), 1978.

Consumer Interests

Alderson, G. and Sentman, E.. *How You Can Influence Congress.* New York: E.P. Dutton, 1979.

Alderson, G. *How to Influence Your Congressman.* From the Voter's Guide to Environmental Politics. FOE/Ballantine (no date), Pp. 1-4.

Anderson, M. "U Workshop Teacher's Tactics: Student Lobbyist to Push Environmental Measures." Ann Arbor, Mich.: *The Michigan Daily*, March 18, 1978.

Blaisdell. The Techniques of Lobbies and Pressure Groups, In *American Democracy Under Pressure*, 1957, Pp. 99-111.

Greever. *Tactical Investigations for People's Struggles.* Copies may be obtained from The Youth Project, 1000 Wisconsin Ave., N.W., Washington, D.C. 20007.

NACLA Research Methodology Guide. New York: North American Congress on Latin America, 1971.

Open the Books: How to Research a Corporation. Braintree, Mass.: Alpine Press, 1974.

Corporate Research

Anderson, D. and Benjaminson, P. *Investigative Reporting.* Bloomington, Ind.: University Press, 1976, Pp. 7-67.

Greever, B. *Tactical Investigations for People's Struggles.* Copies may be obtained from the Youth Project, 1000 Wisconsin Ave., N.W., Washington, D.C. 20007.

How to Read a Financial Report. Merrill, Lynch, Pierce, Fenner, and Smith, Inc., One Liberty Plaza, 165 Broadway, New York (no date).

Kelly, Ed and Webb, L. *Plant Closings, Resources for Public Officials and Activists.* Washington, D.C.: A Publication of the Conference on State and Local Policies, 1901 Que Street, N.W., 1979, Pp. 22-24, 30-35, 52-59.

Kelly, E. and Webb, L. *Tax Abatements: Resources for Public Officials and Activists.* Washington, D.C.: A Publication of the Conference of State and Local Policies, 1901 Que Street, N.W., May 1979, Pp. 11-36, 46-49.

NACLA Research Methodology Guide. New York: North American Congress on Latin America, 1971.

Open the Books: How to Research a Corporation. Braintree, Mass.: Alpine Press, 1974.

Fund Raising

Flanagan, J. *The Grass Roots Fundraising Book: How to Raise Money in Your Community.* Chicago: The Shallow Press, 1977.

Fund Raising in the Public Interest. The NRAG Papers. Helena, Montana: A Publication of the Northern Rockies Action Group, Vol. 1(1), January 1976.

Mitiguy, Nancy. *The Rich Get Richer and the Poor Write Proposals.* University of Mass. (Citizen Involvement Training Project) 1978.

Media/Diffusion Skills

Gordon, Robbie. *We Interrupt This Program...A Citizens Guide to Using the Media for Social Change.* University of Mass. (Citizen Involvement Training Project), 1978.

Prentice, L. *Words, Pictures, and Media: Citizen Action Research for Better Schools.* Boston: Institute for Responsive Education.

Sandman, P. *Persuasion and Communication Theory.* The NRAG Papers. Vol. 1(4), 1976.

Nonviolent Strategies

Conant, R. Rioting, insurrection and civil disobedience. *American Scholar,* 37, 1968, pp. 420-33.

Hoch, S. Seabrook: A Political Community Mobilizes. Reprinted from *Communities: A Journal of Cooperative Living.* Sept./Oct. 1977, Pp. 1-5.

Kurtz, P. Misuses of civil disobedience, *Social Work.* Jan.-Feb., 1970, Pp. 66-74.

Specht, H. Disruptive Tactics, *Social Work.* April 1969, Pp. 5-15.

Political Campaigns

Aronoff, R. *The Management of Election Campaigns.* Boston: Holbrook Press, Inc., 1976.

Greever, B. *Checking on Elected Officials: Questions About Elected Officials and Where To Go to Get Them Answered.* Distributed by the Midwest Academy, 600 W. Fullerton, Chicago, Ill. (no date).

Neustadt, R. and, Paisner R. How to Run on T.V, *New York Times Magazine,* Sec. 6, Dec. 15, 1974. Pp. 20, 72+.

Political Parties in NACLA Methodology Guide. New York: North American Congress on Latin America, 1971.

Soeter, Greg. *Playing Their Game Our Way: Using the Political Process to Meet Community Needs.* University of Mass. (Citizen Involvement Training Project), 1978.

Property Research

Anderson, D. and, Benjamison P. *Investigative Reporting.* Bloomington: Indiana University Press, 1976.

Greever, Barry. *Tactical Investigations for People's Struggles.* Copies may be obtained from The Youth Project, 1000 Wisconsin Avenue, N.W., Washington, D.C. 20007.

People Before Property: A Real Estate Primer and Research Guide. Cambridge, Mass: Urban Planning Aid, Inc., 1972.

Survey Research Skills

Burges, Bill. *A Layman's Guide to Conducting Surveys.* Boston: Institute for Responsive Education, 1976, Pp. 1-61.

Sandman, P. Quick and Easy Research. *The NRAG Papers.* Vol. 1(4), 1976, Pp. 13-18.

References Cited in this Manual

Albelda, R. et al. *Mink Coats Don't Trickle Down .* Boston: South End Press, 1988

Alinsky, S. *Reveille for Radicals.* New York: Vintage Books, 1969.

Alinsky, S. *Rules for Radicals: A Pragmatic Primer for Realistic Radicals.* New York: Vintage Books, 1972.

Bailey, R., Jr. *Radicals in Urban Politics: The Alinsky Approach.* Chicago: The University of Chicago Press, 1974.

Batra, R. *The Great Depression of 1990.* New York: A Dell Book, 1987.

Buttel, F. and Larson, O. W., III. Whither Environmentalism: The Future Political Path of the Environmental Movement, *Natural Resources Journal,* Vol. 20, April 1980.

Catton, W. R., Jr. and Dunlap, R. E. A New Ecological Paradigm for PostExuberant Sociology, *American Behavioral Scientist,* Vol. 24(1), Sept./Oct., 1980.

Corporate Action Guide: A Corporate Action Project. Washington, D.C.: Corporation Action Project, 1975.

Cyper, J. M. The Basic Economics of Rearming America. *Science for the People.* July/Aug. 1981.

Flavin, C. *Worldwatch Paper 75: Reassessing Nuclear Power: The Fallout From Chernobyl.* Washington, D.C.: Worldwatch Institute, 1987.

Folbre, N. (Coordinator) *A Field Guide to the U..S. Economy.* New York: Pantheon Books, 1987.

French, J. R. P., Jr. and Raven, B. The Bases of Power, in Cartwright, D. and Zander, A. (eds.), *Group Dynamics: Research and Theory* (Third Edition). New York: Harper and Row, 1960.

Gamson, W. *The Strategy of Social Protest.* Homewood, Illinois: The Dorsey Press, 1975.

Gordon, R. *We Interrupt This Program.* University of Massachusetts (Citizens Involvement Training Project), 1978.

Jackson, J. *Paying for Our Dreams: A Budget Plan for Jobs, Peace, and Justice.* Chicago: 30 West Washington Street, Suite 300, Zip 60602, 1988.

Joblonski, D. (ed.). *How to Find Information About Companies.* Washington, D.C.: Washington Researchers, 1979.

Law-Yone, W. and Joblonski, D. M. (eds.). *Company Information: A Model Investigation.* Washington, D.C.: Washington Researchers, 1980.

Littlejohn, S. W. Eight Theories of Persuasion, in *Theories of Human Communication.* Belmont, Calf.: Wadsworth, 1983.

Miller, G. T., Jr. *Living in the Environment* (Third Edition). Belmont, Calif.: Wadsworth Publishing Company, 1982.

NACLA Research Methodology Guide. New York: North American Congress on Latin America, 1971.

Olson, M. *The Logic of Collective Action: Public Goods and The Theory of Groups.* Cambridge, Mass: Harvard University Press, 1971.

Robinson, G. The Best Little Citizens Group in Texas, *Environment Action.* May, 1980.

Sandman, P. Mass Media, *The NRAG Papers:* A Publication of the Northern Rockies Action Group. Oct. 1976.

Sharpe, G. *The Politics of Nonviolent Action.* Boston: Porter Sargent, 1973.

Schnaiber, A. Politics, Participation and Pollution: The Environment Movement, in Walton, J. and Carns, D. (eds.) *Cities in Change: A Reader on Urban Sociology.* Boston: Allyn and Bacon, 1973.

Shulman, H. Access to Media, *The NRAG Papers:* A Publication of the Northern Rockies Action Group. Oct. 1976.

U. S. Civil Rights Commission. *The Decline of Black Farming in America.* Washington D.C.: U. S. Government Printing Office, 1982, -0-522-037/7733.

U. S. Department of Commerce, Bureau of the Census, *Poverty in the United States* 1985. Washington D.C.: U. S. Government Printing Office, 1987.

U. S. General Accounting Office, *Siting of Hazardous Waste Landfills and their Correlation with Racial and Economic Status of Surrounding Communities.* Washington D.C.: June 1, 1983, GAO/RCED-83-168.

U. S. Department of Commerce, Bureau of the Census, *Statistical Abstracts of the United States 107 Edition.* Washington D.C.: U.S. Government Printing Office, 1987.

Westin, A. *Whistle Blowing.* New York: McGraw-Hill, 1981.

Weiss, G. America's Most Valuable Companies. *Business Week: Special 1989 Bonus Issue,* 1989.

Appendix Five:

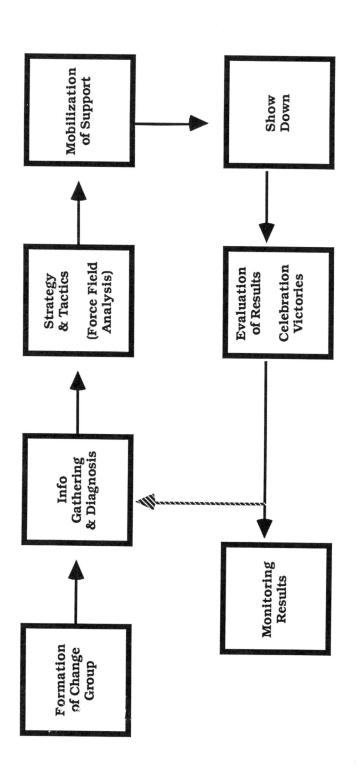

Change Model

If a failure, then the process starts over again.

About the Author

Bunyan Bryant, a faculty member with the School of Natural Resources at The University of Michigan, teaches in the Program of Urban Technological and Environmental Planning. His courses include: "Small Group Organization and Advocacy Planning," "Social Change, Energy, and Land Ethics," and "Social Change and Natural Resources."

Bryant holds a Ph.D. degree in education and a M.S.W. degree in social work, both from The University of Michigan, and a B.S. degree from Eastern Michigan University, where he majored in social science with minors in biology and psychology. He has completed post-graduate study in Town and County Planning at the University of Manchester, England, and has extensive preparation in organizational training and development from the National Training laboratory and Tavistock Laboratory.

While serving as a research director at the Institute for Social Research at The University of Michigan in the late 1960s and early 1970s, Bryant designed and executed action research projects with school systems experiencing racial conflict. During his faculty service with the School of Natural Resources he has concentrated on research evaluation and training for public interest groups and non-profit organizations.

Bryant feels that many educational, environmental, and ecological crises, such as the current difficulties experienced by family farms, are essentially socio-political and economic in character. In exploring such issues, he has served as a volunteer consultant and has encouraged his students to choose alternative careers--ones which will help people organize to improve their educational, environmental, and social conditions.

Bryant's current research interests include developing case studies on corporate, agency, and community responses to toxic dumpsites, and comparing the effectiveness of various telecommunications modes for teaching, training, and organizing.

Other Books by Bunyan Bryant

Also available from **Caddo Gap Press** are:

Quality Circles:
New Management Strategies for Schools
   1987. 85 pages. Paperback. $ 8.95.

Social Change, Energy, and Land Ethics
   1989. 104 pages. Paperback. $9.95.

Environmental Advocacy:
Concepts, Issues, and Dilemmas
   1990. 140 pages. Paperback. $9.95

To order, or for more information, contact:

Caddo Gap Press
1411 West Covell Boulevard
Suite 106-305
Davis, California 95616
(916) 753-1946